Contents

Introduction

This is BPP Learning Media's AAT Question Bank for *Cash and Treasury Management*. It is part of a suite of ground-breaking resources produced by BPP Learning Media for AAT assessments.

This Question Bank has been written in conjunction with the BPP Course Book, and has been carefully designed to enable students to practise all of the learning outcomes and assessment criteria for the units that make up *Cash and Treasury Management*. It is fully up to date as at June 2017 and reflects both the AAT's qualification specification and the sample assessment provided by the AAT.

This Question Bank contains these key features:

- Tasks corresponding to each chapter of the Course Book. Some tasks are designed for learning purposes, others are of assessment standard

- AAT's AQ2016 sample assessment 1 and answers for *Cash and Treasury Management* and further BPP practice assessments

The emphasis in all tasks and assessments is on the practical application of the skills acquired.

VAT

You may find tasks throughout this Question Bank that need you to calculate or be aware of a rate of VAT. This is stated at 20% in these examples and questions.

Approaching the assessment

When you sit the assessment it is very important that you follow the on screen instructions. This means you need to carefully read the instructions, both on the introduction screens and during specific tasks.

When you access the assessment you should be presented with an introductory screen with information similar to that shown below (taken from the introductory screen from one of the AAT's AQ2016 sample assessments for *Cash and Treasury Management*).

We have provided this **sample assessment** to help you familiarise yourself with our e-assessment environment. It is designed to demonstrate as many of the question types that you may find in a live assessment as possible. It is not designed to be used on its own to determine whether you are ready for a live assessment.

At the end of this sample assessment you will receive an immediate assessment result. This will only take into account your responses to tasks 1 - 5, 7 and 9 as these are the elements of the assessment that are computer marked. In the live assessment, your responses to tasks 6, 8 and 10 will be human marked.

Assessment information:

You have **2 hours and 30 minutes** to complete this sample assessment.

This assessment contains **10 tasks** and you should attempt to complete **every** task.
Each task is independent. You will not need to refer to your answers to previous tasks.
Read every task carefully to make sure you understand what is required.

Where the date is relevant, it is given in the task data.
Both minus signs and brackets can be used to indicate negative numbers **unless** task instructions say otherwise.

You must use a full stop to indicate a decimal point. For example, write 100.57 NOT 100,57 or 100 57
You may use a comma to indicate a number in the thousands, but you don't have to. For example, 10000 and 10,000 are both acceptable.

The actual instructions will vary depending on the subject you are studying for. It is very important you read the instructions on the introductory screen and apply them in the assessment. You don't want to lose marks when you know the correct answer just because you have not entered it in the right format.

In general, the rules set out in the AAT sample assessments for the subject you are studying for will apply in the real assessment, but you should carefully read the information on this screen again in the real assessment, just to make sure. This screen may also confirm the VAT rate used if applicable.

A full stop is needed to indicate a decimal point. We would recommend using minus signs to indicate negative numbers and leaving out the comma signs to indicate thousands, as this results in a lower number of key strokes and less margin for error when working under time pressure. Having said that, you can use whatever is easiest for you as long as you operate within the rules set out for your particular assessment.

You have to show competence throughout the assessment and you should therefore complete all of the tasks. Don't leave questions unanswered.

In some assessments, written or complex tasks may be human marked. In this case you are given a blank space or table to enter your answer into. You are told in the assessments which tasks these are (note: there may be none if all answers are marked by the computer).

If these involve calculations, it is a good idea to decide in advance how you are going to lay out your answers to such tasks by practising answering them on a word document, and certainly you should try all such tasks in this Question Bank and in the AAT's environment using the sample assessment.

When asked to fill in tables, or gaps, never leave any blank even if you are unsure of the answer. Fill in your best estimate.

Note that for some assessments where there is a lot of scenario information or tables of data provided (eg tax tables), you may need to access these via 'pop-ups'. Instructions will be provided on how you can bring up the necessary data during the assessment.

Finally, take note of any task specific instructions once you are in the assessment. For example you may be asked to enter a date in a certain format or to enter a number to a certain number of decimal places.

Grading

To achieve the qualification and to be awarded a grade, you must pass all the mandatory unit assessments, all optional unit assessments (where applicable) and the synoptic assessment.

The AAT Level 4 Professional Diploma in Accounting will be awarded a grade. This grade will be based on performance across the qualification. Unit assessments and synoptic assessments are not individually graded. These assessments are given a mark that is used in calculating the overall grade.

How overall grade is determined

You will be awarded an overall qualification grade (Distinction, Merit, and Pass). If you do not achieve the qualification you will not receive a qualification certificate, and the grade will be shown as unclassified.

The marks of each assessment will be converted into a percentage mark and rounded up or down to the nearest whole number. This percentage mark is then weighted according to the weighting of the unit assessment or synoptic assessment within the qualification. The resulting weighted assessment percentages are combined to arrive at a percentage mark for the whole qualification.

Grade definition	Percentage threshold
Distinction	90–100%
Merit	80–89%
Pass	70–79%
Unclassified	0–69% Or failure to pass one or more assessment/s

Re-sits

The AAT Professional Diploma In Accounting is not subject to re-sit restrictions.

You should only be entered for an assessment when you are well prepared and you expect to pass the assessment.

AAT qualifications

The material in this book may support the following AAT qualifications:

AAT Professional Diploma in Accounting Level 4, AAT Professional Diploma in Accounting at SCQF Level 8 and Certificate: Accounting (Level 5 AATSA).

Supplements

From time to time we may need to publish supplementary materials to one of our titles. This can be for a variety of reasons. From a small change in the AAT unit guidance to new legislation coming into effect between editions.

You should check our supplements page regularly for anything that may affect your learning materials. All supplements are available free of charge on our supplements page on our website at:

www.bpp.com/learning-media/about/students

Improving material and removing errors

There is a constant need to update and enhance our study materials in line with both regulatory changes and new insights into the assessments.

From our team of authors BPP appoints a subject expert to update and improve these materials for each new edition.

Their updated draft is subsequently technically checked by another author and from time to time non-technically checked by a proof reader.

We are very keen to remove as many numerical errors and narrative typos as we can but given the volume of detailed information being changed in a short space of time we know that a few errors will sometimes get through our net.

We apologise in advance for any inconvenience that an error might cause. We continue to look for new ways to improve these study materials and would welcome your suggestions. If you have any comments about this book, please email nisarahmed@bpp.com or write to Nisar Ahmed, AAT Head of Programme, BPP Learning Media Ltd, BPP House, Aldine Place, London W12 8AA.

Question Bank

Chapter 1 – Cash flow and profit

Task 1.1

Selecting from the picklists, complete the following sentences.

If a business makes a profit this means that [⬇]

Picklist:

its cash inflows are greater than its cash outflow.
its revenue is greater than its expenses.

Cash flow and profit will [⬇] be the same figure for a period.

Picklist:

normally
not normally

Task 1.2

Give five reasons why there might be a difference between the profit of a business and its cash balance.

1

2

3

4

5

Task 1.3

Given below is the forecast statement of profit or loss for a business for the three months ending 31 December together with forecast statements of financial position at that date and also at the previous 30 September.

Forecast statement of profit or loss for the three months ending 31 December

	£000
Revenue	860
Cost of sales	(600)
Gross profit	260
Depreciation	(20)
Overheads	(100)
Profit from operations	140

Forecast statements of financial position

	31 December £000	£000	30 September £000	£000
Non-current assets		1,050		760
Current assets:				
Inventory	100		100	
Receivables	85		45	
Cash	10		10	
	195		155	
Payables	100		75	
Accruals of overheads	45		40	
	145		115	

	31 December £000	£000	30 September £000	£000
Net current assets		50		40
		1,100		800
Equity share capital		600		600
Retained earnings		500		200
		1,100		800

Calculate the actual cash receipts and cash payments for the quarter to 31 December.

	£000
Sales receipts	
Purchase payments	
Overhead payments	

Task 1.4

The carrying amount of non-current assets on 1 January was £125,000 and the statement of financial position at 31 December shows non-current assets of £152,000. During the year £12,500 depreciation was charged. There were no non-current asset disposals.

What was the cash paid to acquire non-current assets in the year ended 31 December?

	✓
£12,500	
£14,500	
£27,000	
£39,500	

Task 1.5

A business decides to sell one of its buildings which originally cost £105,000 and on which, at the date of disposal, accumulated depreciation amounted to £48,500. The sale generated a profit on disposal of £35,000.

What were the cash proceeds on disposal of the building?

	✓
£21,500	
£56,500	
£70,000	
£91,500	

Task 1.6

The following information has been extracted from the Sales Ledger Control Account for the year ended 31 July:

	£
Opening trade receivables	34,500
Closing trade receivables	47,900
Sales revenue per statement of profit or loss	252,000

Sales revenue per statement of profit or loss		34,500
Closing trade receivables		47,900
Opening trade receivables		252,000

Drag and drop the descriptions and figures above to the correct place in the control account then complete the account to determine the cash received from customers during the year:

Sales Ledger Control Account

	Dr £		Cr £
		Cash received	

Chapter 2 – Forecasting income and expenditure

Task 2.1

Given below are the daily takings in a shop that is open five days a week, Monday to Friday.

	Mon £	Tues £	Wed £	Thurs £	Fri £
Week 1	1,260	1,600	1,630	1,780	1,830
Week 2	1,340	1,750	1,640	1,850	1,980
Week 3	1,550	1,660	1,620	1,870	1,970

Calculate the five-day moving average for the daily takings.

Week	Day	Takings £	Five-day moving average £

Task 2.2

In time series analysis there are a number of elements of a time series.

Match each element of a time series analysis listed on the left with its correct description from the list on the right.

| Random variation | Variations in the time series due to the seasonality of the business |

| Trend | Long-term variations caused by general economic factors |

| Cyclical variation | Other variations not due to the trend, cyclical or seasonal variations |

| Seasonal variation | General movement in the time series figure |

Task 2.3

A company is trying to estimate its sales volumes for the first three months of next year. This is to be done by calculating a trend using the actual monthly sales volumes for the current year and a 3-point moving average.

(a) Complete the table below to calculate the monthly sales volume trend and identify any monthly variations.

	Sales volume Units	Trend Units	Monthly variation (volume less trend) Units
January	20,000		
February	17,400		
March	16,300		
April	22,400		
May	19,800		
June	18,700		
July	24,800		
August	22,200		
September	21,100		
October	27,200		
November	24,600		
December	23,500		

The monthly sales volume trend is [   ] units.

(b) **Using the trend and the monthly variations identified in part (a) complete the table below for forecast sales volume for January, February and March of the next financial year.**

	Forecast trend Units	Variation Units	Forecast sales volume Units
January			
February			
March			

Task 2.4

Trend values for sales of barbecues by Hothouse Ltd over the last three years have been as follows:

Year	1st quarter	2nd quarter	3rd quarter	4th quarter
1	7,494	7,665	7,890	8,123
2	8,295	8,493	8,701	8,887
3	9,090	9,296	9,501	9,705

Average seasonal variations for the four quarters have been:

Quarter 1 + 53
Quarter 2 + 997
Quarter 3 + 1,203
Quarter 4 – 2,253

Use the trend and estimates of seasonal variations to forecast sales in each quarter of next year and the associated revenue if the selling price is expected to be £45 per barbecue.

Average increase in trend value [   ] units

Future trend values

Quarter 1 [   ] units
Quarter 2 [   ] units
Quarter 3 [   ] units
Quarter 4 [   ] units

Quarter	Trend forecast	Average seasonal variation	Forecast of actual sales units	Forecast revenue £
1				
2				
3				
4				

Task 2.5

A business currently sells its product for £30 but it is anticipated that there will be a price increase of 4% from 1 February. The sales quantities are expected to be as follows:

January	21,000 units
February	22,000 units
March	22,800 units

All sales are on credit and 40% of cash is received in the month following the sale and the remainder two months after the sale.

What are the receipts from sales that are received in March?

	£
January sales	
February sales	
Total March receipts	

Task 2.6

A business has production overheads of £347,000 in December 20X8 but it is anticipated that these will increase by 1.25% per month for the next few months. Overheads are paid the month after they are incurred.

What is the cash outflow for overheads that is paid during the month of March 20X9 (to the nearest whole £)?

	✓
£347,000	
£355,729	
£351,338	
£360,176	

Task 2.7

A business makes purchases of a raw material which has a cost of £2.60 per kg in November 20X8. The actual and estimated price index for this material is as follows:

	Price index
November (actual)	166.3
December (estimate)	169.0
January (estimate)	173.4
February (estimate)	177.2

What is the expected price per kg (to the nearest penny) of the raw material in each of the months of December, January and February?

	£
December	
January	
February	

Task 2.8

A company, which is growing, has prepared the following regression equation as a basis for estimating sales (Y) in units for the relevant period (X).

$Y = 27X - 24$

Quarterly seasonal variations affecting sales levels are as follows.

Q1	Q2	Q3	Q4
−25%	−25%	+15%	+35%

Period 12 is in Quarter 4.

What is the forecast sales level for period 12?

Forecast P12 sales [   ] units

Task 2.9

Explain possible methods of forecasting sales, making appropriate reference to the use of statistical techniques.

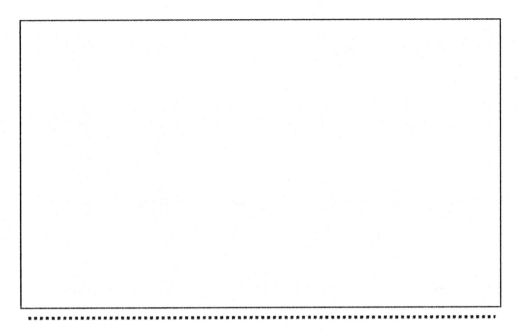

Task 2.10

(a) A company uses time series analysis and regression techniques to estimate future sales demand. Using these techniques, it has derived the following trend equation:

$y = 10,000 + 4,200x$

where y is the total sales units; and

x is the time period

It has also derived the following seasonal variation index values for each of the quarters using the multiplicative seasonal variation model:

Quarter	Index value
1	120
2	80
3	95
4	105

What are the total sales units that will be forecast for time period 33, which is the first quarter of year 9?

| | units

(b) Time series analysis and regression techniques are based on extrapolations of past performance into the future in order to provide information for planning and decision making.

Discuss the problems of extrapolating past performance into the future.

Chapter 3 – Patterns of cash flows

Task 3.1

Cash receipts and payments take many different forms which may include regular receipts and payments, irregular receipts and payments, capital payments and drawings/dividends.

Complete the table by dragging and dropping the appropriate example to match the correct type of cash receipt or cash payment.

Type of receipt/payment	Example
Regular revenue receipts	
Regular revenue payments	
Exceptional receipts/payments	
Capital payments/receipts	
Drawings/dividends	

The drag and drop choices are:

Income received from HM Revenue and Customs

Income received from the operating activities of the business which are expected to occur frequently

Income received from the operating activities of the business which are not expected to occur frequently

Income received from the owner of the business

Income that arises from the proceeds of the sale of non-current assets

Payments due to the operating activities of the business that are expected to be incurred frequently

Payments due to the operating activities of the business that are not expected to be incurred frequently

Payments made to the owner of the business

Payments that arise from the acquisition of non-current assets

Task 3.2

A business makes 30% of its monthly sales for cash with the remainder being sold on credit. On average 40% of the total sales are received in the month following the sale and the remainder in the second month after the sale. Sales figures are estimated to be as follows.

	£
August	240,000
September	265,000
October	280,000
November	250,000
December	220,000

What are the cash receipts from sales that are received in each of the three months from October to December? Round to the nearest whole £.

Cash Sales	October £	November £	December £
Cash Sales			
October			
November			
December			
Credit sales			
August			
September			
September			
October			
October			
November			
Total cash receipts			

Task 3.3

A business purchases all of its goods on credit from suppliers. 20% of purchases are offered a discount of 2% for payment in the month of purchase and the business takes advantage of these discounts. A further 45% of purchases are paid for in the month after the purchase and the remainder are paid for two months after the purchase. Purchases figures are estimated to be as follows.

	£
August	180,000
September	165,000
October	190,000
November	200,000
December	220,000

What are the cash payments made to suppliers in each of the three months from October to December? Round to the nearest whole £.

	October £	November £	December £

Task 3.4

A retail business buys flowers from a wholesaler, adds a mark-up of 50% on cost and then sells them to its customers, in the month of purchase, for cash.

If purchases for the three months from January to March are as follows, what are the monthly cash sales? Round to the nearest whole £.

	January £	February £	March £
Purchases	22,000	24,000	26,000
Cash sales			

The margin that the retailer is making is ☐ %.

....

Task 3.5

A business makes all of its sales on credit with a 3% settlement discount offered for payment within the month of the sale. 25% of sales take up this settlement discount and 70% of sales are paid in the following month. The remainder are irrecoverable debts.

Sales figures are as follows.

	£
March	650,000
April	600,000
May	580,000
June	550,000

(a) **What are the cash receipts from sales that are received in each of the three months from April to June? Round to the nearest whole £.**

	April £	May £	June £
Total cash receipts			

The business is considering the effect of increasing the settlement discount to 5%. As a result, with effect from March sales, 30% of customers are expected to take the discount and all remaining customers to pay in the following month, with no irrecoverable debts.

(b) **What are the revised cash receipts from sales? Round to the nearest whole £.**

	April £	May £	June £
Total cash receipts			

Task 3.6

(a) A company's trade receivables balance at the beginning of the year was £22,000. The statement of profit or loss showed revenue from credit sales of £290,510 during the year. The trade receivables days at the end of the year were 49 days.

Assume that:

- Sales occur evenly throughout the year
- All balances outstanding at the start of the year were received
- All sales are on credit and there were no irrecoverable debts
- No trade discount was given

How much cash did the company receive from its customers during the year?

£ [   ]

(b) A company has a balance outstanding on its trade receivables account at the start of the year of £83,000 after allowing for irrecoverable debts. The company forecasts sales revenue for the next year of £492,750. All sales are on credit.

Based on past experience, irrecoverable debts represent 5% of sales revenue. Trade receivable days at the end of the year are expected to be 60 days.

What are the expected cash receipts from customers during the year (to the nearest penny)?

£ [   ]

··

Task 3.7

A company, CTF Co is expected to receive some foreign currency receipts as follows:

1 January	NOK350,000 (krone) from a Norwegian customer
1 February	$230,000 from a US customer
1 March	SFr150,000 from a Swiss customer
1 April	€450,000 from a French customer

The expected exchange rates are as follows:

1 January	1NOK:£0.086
1 February	£1:$1.58
1 March	£1:SFr1.44
1 April	€1:£0.72

Calculate the expected receipts in £. Give your answers to two decimal places.

Month	Receipt £
January	
February	
March	
April	

Task 3.8

A business manufactures and sells a single product, each unit of which requires 20 minutes of labour. The wage rate is £8.40 per hour. The production budget is anticipated to be:

	April	May	June	July
Sales in units	7,200	7,050	6,450	6,000

The product is produced one month prior to sale and wages are paid in the month of production.

Calculate the cash payments for wages for each of the three months from April to June.

Labour budget – hours	May Hours	June Hours	July Hours
May			
June			
July			
Labour budget – £	**April £**	**May £**	**June £**
April			
May			
June			

Chapter 4 – Preparing cash budgets

Task 4.1

A company pays interest at 13% per annum on its overdraft.

Two of the company's suppliers, X and Y are offering the following terms for immediate cash settlement.

Company	Discount	Normal settlement period
X	3%	3 months
Y	4%	4 months

(a) **Which of the following discounts should be accepted?**

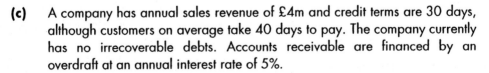

Picklist:

Both X and Y
Neither X nor Y
X only
Y only

The company is also concerned about the increasing level of trade receivables and is considering various options to encourage customers to pay earlier. The company currently offers 30 day payment terms but customers are taking on average 65 days to pay.

One option being considered is to offer an early settlement discount of 2.5% for customers paying within 15 days.

(b) **Calculate, to the nearest 0.1%, the effective annual interest rate to the company of offering this discount if all customers pay within 15 days. You should assume a 365 day year and use compound interest methodology.**

(c) A company has annual sales revenue of £4m and credit terms are 30 days, although customers on average take 40 days to pay. The company currently has no irrecoverable debts. Accounts receivable are financed by an overdraft at an annual interest rate of 5%.

The company plans to offer an early settlement discount of 2% for payment within 10 days and to extend the maximum credit offered to 60 days. The company expects that these changes will increase annual credit sales by 8%. The gross profit margin on sales is 50% and the change in credit policy

will give rise to additional administration costs, equal to 1% of total sales revenue. The discount is expected to be taken by 25% of customers, with the remaining customers taking an average of 50 days to pay. There will be no irrecoverable debts.

Evaluate the impact of the proposed changes in credit policy on profitability.

Task 4.2

A manufacturing company is preparing its cash budget for the three months ending 31 July. The production budget is estimated to be as follows.

	April	May	June	July	August
Production quantity	1,020	1,220	1,320	1,520	1,620

The materials required for the product are 2 kg per unit costing £40 per kg and are purchased in the month prior to production and paid for in the following month. At 1 April there are 550 kgs of raw material in inventory but these are to be reduced by 50 kgs per month for each of the next four months.

(a) **Use the table below to complete the purchases budget in kgs and £s for April to July**

	April kgs	May kgs	June kgs	July kgs
Materials required for production				
April				
May				
June				
July				
Opening inventory				
Closing inventory				
Purchases in kgs				

	April £	May £	June £	July £
April				
May				
June				
July				

(b) **Calculate the cash payments to suppliers for May to July**

	May £	June £	July £
Cash payments			

Task 4.3

A business is about to prepare a cash budget for the quarter ending 30 September. The recent actual and estimated sales figures are as follows.

	£
April (actual)	420,000
May (actual)	400,000
June (estimate)	480,000
July (estimate)	500,000
August (estimate)	520,000
September (estimate)	510,000

All sales are on credit and the payment pattern is as follows.
20% pay in the month of sale after taking a 4% settlement discount.
40% pay in the month following the sale.
25% pay two months after the month of sale.
12% pay three months after the month of sale.
There are expected to be 3% irrecoverable debts.

(a) **Complete the table below to show the cash receipts from customers.**

	Workings	July £	August £	September £
April sales				
May sales				
June sales				
July sales				

	Workings	July £	August £	September £
August sales				
September sales				
Total receipts				

The purchases of the business are all on credit and it is estimated that the following purchases will be made.

	£
May	250,000
June	240,000
July	280,000
August	300,000
September	310,000

40% of purchases are paid for in the month after the purchase has been made and the remainder are paid for two months after the month of purchase.

(b) Complete the table below to show the cash payments to suppliers.

	Workings	July £	August £	September £
May purchases				
June purchases				
July purchases				
August purchases				
Total payments				

General overheads are anticipated to be a monthly £50,000 for June and July increasing to £55,000 thereafter. 75% of the general overheads are paid in the month in which they are incurred and the remainder in the following month. The general overheads figure includes a depreciation charge of £6,000 each month.

(c) **Complete the table below to show the cash payments for general overheads.**

	Workings	July £	August £	September £
June overheads				
July overheads				
August overheads				
September overheads				
Total overhead payments				

Additional information

- Wages are expected to be £60,000 each month and are paid in the month in which they are incurred.

- Selling expenses are expected to be 10% of the monthly sales value and are paid for in the month following the sale.

- The business has planned to purchase new equipment for £42,000 in August and in the same month to dispose of old equipment with estimated sales proceeds of £7,500.

- Overdraft interest is charged at 1% per month based on the overdraft balance at the start of the month. At 1 July it is anticipated that the business will have an overdraft of £82,000.

(d) **Referring to your answers in parts (a), (b) and (c) and the additional information above, prepare a monthly cash budget for the three months ending September. Cash inflows should be entered as positive figures and cash outflows as negative figures. Zeros must be entered where appropriate to achieve full marks.**

	July £	August £	September £
Receipts			
Receipts from credit sales			
Proceeds from sale of equipment			
Total receipts			
Payments			
Payments to suppliers			
Wages			
Overheads			
Selling expenses			
Equipment			
Overdraft interest			
Total payments			
Net cash flow			
Opening balance			
Closing balance			

Task 4.4

A manufacturing business is to prepare its cash budget for the three months ending 31 December. The business manufactures a single product which requires 3 kg of raw material per unit and three hours of labour per unit. Production is in the month of sale. The raw material cost is anticipated to be £9 per kg and the labour force is paid at a rate of £7.20 per hour. Each unit of the product sells for £75.

The forecast sales in units are as follows:

	August	September	October	November	December
Forecast sales – units	5,000	5,100	5,400	5,800	6,000

Sales are on credit with 40% of customers paying the month after sale and the remainder two months after the sale.

(a) **Complete the table below to calculate the timing of receipts from credit customers to be included in the cash budget.**

	Workings	October £	November £	December £
August sales				
September sales				
October sales				
November sales				
Total cash receipts				

The raw materials required for production are purchased in the month prior to production and 60% are paid for in the following month and the remainder two months after purchase. The anticipated inventory of raw materials is 3,000 kgs until the end of September and the planned inventory levels at the end of each month thereafter are as follows:

October 3,200 kgs
November 3,500 kgs
December 4,000 kgs

The production budget is as follows:	August Units	September Units	October Units	November Units	December Units
Production	5,000	5,100	5,500	5,900	6,100

(b) **Complete the following table to give the purchases budget for August to November in both kgs and £.**

	August kg	September kg	October kg	November kg
Kgs required for production				
Opening inventory				
Closing inventory				
Purchases in kgs				
	£	£	£	£
Purchases in £				

(c) **Using the information from part (b) and above complete the following table to calculate the payments to suppliers for October to December.**

	Workings	October £	November £	December £
August purchases				
September purchases				
October purchases				
November purchases				
Total cash payments				

Wages are paid in the month in which they are incurred.

(d) **Complete the table below to show the labour budget for October to December in hours and in £.**

	October Hours	November Hours	December Hours
Production times hours per unit			
	£	£	£
Production hours times wage rate			

Additional information

- Production overheads are expected to be £60,000 each month and are paid for in the month in which they are incurred. This figure includes depreciation of £10,000 per month for machinery.

- General overheads are anticipated to be £72,000 each month in October and November increasing to £80,000 in December and are paid in the month in which they are incurred. The figure for general overheads includes £12,000 of depreciation each month.

- The cash balance at 1 October is expected to be £40,000 in credit.

(e) **Referring to your answers in parts (a) to (d) and the additional information above, prepare a monthly cash budget for the three months ending December. Cash inflows should be entered as positive figures and cash outflows as negative figures. Zeroes must be entered where appropriate to achieve full marks.**

	October £	November £	December £
Receipts			
From credit customers			
Payments			
To credit suppliers			
Wages			
Production overheads			
General overheads			
Total payments			
Net cash flow			
Opening bank balance			
Closing bank balance			

Task 4.5

A business currently pays its suppliers with the following pattern:

60% one month after the date of purchase
40% two months after the date of purchase

On 30% of these purchases a 3% discount is offered for payment during the month of purchase but in the past the business has not taken advantage of this. If it did take advantage then 30% of purchases would be paid for in the month of purchase, 40% in the month following purchase and 30% two months after the date of purchase.

Purchases are estimated to be as follows:

	£
August	520,000
September	550,000
October	560,000
November	580,000
December	600,000

(a) **Using the table below calculate the payments to suppliers in October, November and December in accordance with the current situation where no settlement discounts are taken.**

	Workings	October £	November £	December £
August purchases				
September purchases				
October purchases				
November purchases				
Total cash payments				

(b) **Using the table below calculate the payments made to suppliers in October, November and December in accordance with the new settlement discount scheme described above on the assumption that the scheme begins in October.**

	Workings	October £	November £	December £
August purchases				
September purchases				
October purchases				
November purchases				
December purchases				
Total cash payments				

Task 4.6

At 31 March a business had receivables of £260,000. Planned sales for the following three months in units are:

April	140,000 units
May	150,000 units
June	155,000 units

All sales are made on credit. On average 40% of receivables pay during the month after the sale and the remainder pay two months after the date of sale.

The receivables at 31 March can be assumed to pay as follows:

	£
In April	140,000
In May	120,000
	260,000

Sales are made at a price of £1.00 per unit.

However, in the light of current economic circumstances it is being anticipated that the sales price will have to be reduced to £0.90 per unit.

(a) **Use the table below to calculate the effect of the changes in the forecast amounts for April, May and June.**

	April £	May £	June £
Original value of forecast sales			
Original timing of receipts			
Revised value of forecast sales			
Revised timing of receipts			
Increase/(decrease) in sales receipts			

An extract from the original cash budget is set out below.

	April £	May £	June £
Net cash flow	(12,000)	40,000	44,000
Opening bank balance	(20,000)	(32,000)	8,000
Closing bank balance	(32,000)	8,000	52,000

(b) **Using your calculation of the revised receipts in (a) above, complete the table to show the impact of the change in the forecast amounts on the budgeted bank balances.**

	April £	May £	June £
Original net cash flow	(12,000)	40,000	44,000
Increase/(decrease) in sales receipts per (a)			
Revised net cash flow			
Opening bank balance			
Closing bank balance			

Task 4.7

A company is considering its sales budget for the next year. It is expected that sales will be 20,000 units at a selling price of £3.00 per unit. Variable costs are expected to be £1.65 per unit, while fixed costs are expected to be £20,000 per year.

The company wants to know how much flexibility it has to offer discounts on the sales price.

(a) **Explain how sensitivity analysis can help the company to decide on its plans.**

(b) **Calculate the sensitivity of the company's profits to a change in each of the following variables. Express your answer as a % to the nearest 2 decimal places:**

(i) Sales volume ┌─────────────┐

(ii) Sales price ┌─────────────┐

(iii) Variable costs ┌─────────────┐

Task 4.8

A company is preparing its cash budget for the next quarter. In October the quarterly sales tax (VAT) payment relating to June, July and August, is to be paid. Standard rated sales for the three months were £2,125,000 and standard rated purchases were £1,975,000. (Standard rate VAT is 20%.).

How much VAT will be due to HM Revenue and Customs in October?

┌─────────────┐

Task 4.9

A company manufactures and sells a single product. The company is preparing its cash budget for next year. The company divides the year into four periods, each of thirteen weeks. Sales and production will occur evenly within each period. Details are as follows:

Sales budget (810,000 units)

The selling price is £30 per unit. All sales will be on credit and payment will be received five weeks after the date of sale. It is expected that 2% of all sales will become irrecoverable debts. The budgeted sales units are:

Period	1	2	3	4
Sales (units)	150,000	200,000	180,000	280,000

The product incurs variable selling costs of £1.60 per unit. These are paid in the period in which they are incurred.

Production budget (860,000 units)

Period	1	2	3	4
Production (units)	210,000	210,000	220,000	220,000

Production cost per unit

	£	Notes
Raw materials	9.50	Purchased on credit. Paid for four weeks after purchase. See below.
Production wages	8.20	Paid one week in arrears. These are variable costs.
Production expenses	7.00	See below.
Total cost per unit	**24.70**	

Raw material inventory

The company wishes to increase inventory to cover six weeks of future production by the end of Period 1 and then to seven weeks by the end of Period 2. Purchases will occur evenly throughout each period.

Production expenses

The production expenses of £7.00 per unit comprise the following:

	£	Notes
Variable production expenses	1.10	Paid in the period incurred.
Fixed production expenses:		
Depreciation	2.70	This is an annual fixed cost that is absorbed on a per unit basis over the budgeted production of 860,000 units.
Other fixed expenses	3.20	Cost per unit based on the annual production of 860,000 units. Fixed expenses are paid in two equal instalments at the beginning of periods 1 and 3.

Long term borrowing

The company has a long term loan. The balance on this loan at the start of the year will be £10m. Interest on this loan is charged at 9% per annum on the amount outstanding at the start of the year. It is to be paid in two equal instalments at the end of Period 2 and at the end of Period 4. The loan is 'interest only' – there are no capital repayments due.

Opening balances

	£	Notes
Raw materials inventory	710,000	(all purchased at the current price)
Trade receivables	2,430,000	(net of irrecoverable debts)
Bank and cash	76,000	
Trade payables	612,000	
Unpaid wages	130,000	
Loan	10,000,000	

Prepare, showing all cash flows to the nearest £000, a cash budget for Period 1 and Period 2. Use brackets or minus signs where appropriate.

	Period 1 £000	Period 2 £000
Sales receipts		
Raw material purchases		
Production wages		
Variable production expenses		
Variable selling expenses		
Fixed production expenses		
Interest		
Net cash flow for the period		
Opening cash balance		
Closing cash balance		

Chapter 5 – Monitoring cash flows

Task 5.1

Given below is the cash budget for the month of June for a business together with the actual cash flows for the month of June.

Cash budget June	Budget £	Actual £
Receipts:		
Cash sales receipts	101,000	94,000
Credit sales receipts	487,000	475,000
Total receipts	588,000	569,000
Payments:		
Credit suppliers	(303,000)	(294,000)
Wages	(155,000)	(162,000)
Variable overheads	(98,600)	(99,400)
Fixed overheads	(40,000)	(40,000)
Capital expenditure	–	(45,000)
Total payments	(596,600)	(640,400)
Net cash flow for the month	(8,600)	(71,400)
Bank b/f	20,300	20,300
Bank c/f	11,700	(51,100)

Complete the table below to compare the actual cash flows to the budgeted cash flows and identify any variances indicating whether they are favourable or adverse variances.

	Budget £	Actual £	Variance £	Adv/Fav £
Receipts:				
Cash sales receipts				
Credit sales receipts				
Total receipts				
Payments:				
Credit suppliers				
Wages				
Variable overheads				
Fixed overheads				
Capital expenditure				
Total payments				
Net cash flow				
Balance b/f				
Balance c/f				

Task 5.2

Given below is the cash budget and actual cash flows for a business for the month of July.

	Budget £	Actual £
Receipts:		
Cash sales	264,000	277,000
Receipts from credit customers	888,000	863,000
Proceeds from sale of non-current assets	–	22,000
Total receipts	**1,152,000**	**1,162,000**
Payments:		
Payments to credit suppliers	742,000	777,000
Wages	197,000	197,000
Variable overheads	51,300	58,700
Fixed overheads	66,000	68,000
Purchase of non-current assets	–	46,000
Dividend payment	50,000	50,000
Total payments	**1,106,300**	**1,196,700**
Net cash flow	**45,700**	**(34,700)**
Opening cash balance	16,200	16,200
Closing cash balance	61,900	(18,500)

(a) **Reconcile the budgeted cash balance at 31 July to the actual cash balance at that date using the table below. Select the appropriate description for each entry. Clearly indicate whether figures are to be added or deducted in the reconciliation by entering minus signs where appropriate.**

	£
Budgeted closing bank balance	
Surplus/shortfall in cash sales	
Surplus/shortfall in credit sales receipts	
Increase/decrease in proceeds from sales from non-current assets	
Increase/decrease/no change in payments to credit suppliers	
Increase/decrease in wages	
Increase/decrease in variable overheads	
Increase/decrease in fixed overheads	
Increase/decrease in purchase of non-current assets	
Increase/decrease/no change in dividend payments	
Actual closing bank balance	

(b) **What actions could have been taken to avoid the use of overdraft finance by the end of the month?**

	✓
Delay capital expenditure	
Chase customers to pay sooner	
Delay payments to suppliers	
Marketing campaign to increase sales	

Task 5.3

(a) A business is in the process of comparing its budgeted and actual cash flows for February.

Complete the table below to identify any variances indicating whether they are favourable (+) or adverse (–) variances.

	Budget February £	Actual February £	Variance £
Cash receipts:			
Receipts from sales	148,800	145,600	
Deposit account interest	100	100	
Total cash receipts	**148,900**	**145,700**	
Cash payments:			
Payments to suppliers	–41,600	–56,000	
Salaries	–43,000	–45,150	
Administration overheads	–30,000	–30,000	
Capital expenditure	–20,000	–6,000	
Total payments	**–134,600**	**–137,150**	
Net cash flow	**14,300**	**8,550**	
Opening cash balance	–25,900	–25,900	
Closing cash balance	**–11,600**	**–17,350**	

(b) **Reconcile the budgeted cash balance at end February to the actual cash balance at that date using the table below. Select the appropriate description for each entry. Clearly indicate whether figures are to be added or deducted in the reconciliation by entering minus signs where appropriate.**

	£
Budgeted closing bank balance	
Surplus/shortfall in sales receipts	
Surplus/shortfall/no change in deposit account interest	
Increase/decrease in payments to credit suppliers	
Increase/decrease in salaries	
Increase/decrease/no change in administration overheads	
Increase/decrease in capital expenditure	
Actual closing bank balance	

(c) **From the picklist below, choose the appropriate explanations for the variances identified.**

Sales receipts (Adverse)	▼

Payments to suppliers (Adverse)	▼

Salaries (Adverse)	▼

Capital expenditure (Adverse)	▼

Picklist:

Bonus paid to staff
Cut back on overtime working
Increase in suppliers' prices
Increase product selling price
Issued less share capital
Loss of customers
Negotiated credit with supplier of equipment, provided initial deposit paid in month of purchase
Used up material from inventory

Task 5.4

Variances between actual cash flows and budgeted cash flows can be due to a variety of reasons. There are also a number of courses of action which are available to minimise the effect of adverse variances and to capitalise on the benefit of favourable variances.

Match each variance listed on the left with a possible course of action from the list on the right.

Adverse wages cost variance	Continue to take supplier discounts
Adverse credit sales receipts variance	Schedule less overtime
Favourable credit supplier payments variance	Delay capital expenditure
Adverse capital expenditure variance	Offer settlement discounts for early payment

Task 5.5

(a) Actual payments for overheads in a period were £27,500 and there was an adverse overhead expenditure variance of £1,200.

What was the budgeted figure for overheads?

£ _____

(b) In April a business actually spent £18,000 on the purchase of a non-current asset, giving rise to a favourable variance of £2,300.

How much did the business budget for the cost of the non-current asset?

£ _____

Task 5.6

You are provided with the following information about cash flow relating to a new product in the first month of its launch.

	Budget	Actual
Sales (units)	72,000	64,000
Selling price	£10 per unit	£8.40 per unit
Cash received from sales	£720,000	£430,080

(a) **Calculate the following variances, indicating if each is adverse (Adv) or favourable (Fav).**

	Budget	Actual	Variance	Adv/Fav
Sales (units)	72,000	64,000		
Selling price (£ per unit)	£10 per unit	£8.40 per unit		
Cash received from sales (£)	£720,000	£430,080		

(b) **Comment briefly on the possible causes of a variance.**

(c) Explain the major benefit of analysing variances.

(d) Briefly explain three factors that you would consider before deciding to investigate a variance.

Task 5.7

'Variance analysis presents results after the actual events have taken place and therefore it is of little use to management for planning and control purposes, particularly in a modern manufacturing environment'.

Discuss the above statement.

Task 5.8

The table below relates to online exams which can be purchased and taken after studying a free online course. The figures have been provided by the finance team on the actual receipts and payments from the last monthly reporting period against budget.

The following information has been provided by a colleague:

- The end of course exam fee has been increased from £45 per test to £50 per exam and this has not been taken into account in the budgeted figures.

- There has been a recent increase in the bank base rate from 1.25% to 1.75%.

- To write a new set of exam questions, the department employed a large number of temporary workers.

- It is company policy to ignore variances that are within 10% of budget.

	Budgeted £	Actual £
Receipts:		
Cash sales from exams	4,000,000	4,480,000
Investment income	60,000	69,000
Total receipts	4,060,000	4,549,000
Payments:		
Wages and salaries	(1,150,000)	(1,380,000)
Capital expenditure	(160,000)	(165,000)
Bank charges	(17,000)	(16,090)
Utility costs	(51,000)	(54,000)
Total payments	(1,378,000)	(1,615,090)
Net cash flow	2,682,000	2,933,910

Prepare a report for the Board of Directors which explains why the adverse variances in excess of 10% of the budget could have occurred. Your report should also include:

- **The percentage change in the variances**

- **Possible actions that could be taken to rectify these variances and to reduce the likelihood of recurrence**

Chapter 6 – Liquidity management

Task 6.1

You work in a small business which installs fire alarms. As the only member of the accounts department, you report directly to the proprietor, Mr Blaze. One day, you find the following long note from Mr Blaze on your table.

'I've been to the bank and asked them to lend me some money. I've always had money in the bank, but because the loan is to acquire some new equipment, the bank wants a full set of financial statements. The manager asked for statements of profit or loss and a statement of cash flows. He then started jabbering on in jargon I didn't understand: something about *cash operating cycle times*, as he said they were relevant. I also said we were a profitable business. Then he said he needed some ideas as to how *liquid* we are. I said we were a solid company; we've been trading for many years. He said I'd better chat to an accountant. Please help!'

Choose from the picklists to complete the following sentences.

The cash operating cycle time is the [▼]

Picklist:

inventory holding period plus trade receivables' collection period less trade payables' payment period.
period between cash being paid for purchases and cash received for sales.

Liquid assets include [▼]

Picklist:

cash and non-current assets.
cash and short-term investments.
cash, receivables and inventory.

....

Task 6.2

Kitten Ltd buys raw materials on three months' credit, holds them in store for four months and then issues them to production. The production cycle is a couple of days, and then finished goods are held for one month before they are sold. Credit customers are normally allowed two months' credit.

What is Kitten Ltd's cash operating cycle in months?

	✓
1 month	
2 months	
3 months	
4 months	

Task 6.3

During the year ending 30 June a business had a cash operating cycle of 87 days. It had a trade receivables' collection period of 77 days and trade payables' payment period of 41 days.

What is the inventory holding period of the business, in days?

	✓
31 days	
36 days	
46 days	
51 days	

Task 6.4

A business has a cash operating cycle of 76 days. This is based on an inventory holding period of 65 days, trade receivables' collection period of 55 days and trade payables' payment period of 44 days. The Finance Director of the business wants to improve this.

Which of the following will have the effect of shortening the cash operating cycle of the business?

	✓
Taking advantage of early settlement discounts offered by suppliers	
Offering an early settlement discount to customers	
Increasing the cash balance held in the business's current account	
Increasing the credit terms offered to customers from 30 days to 60 days	

Task 6.5

A business has an inventory holding period of 45 days, trade receivables' collection period of 40 days and trade payables' payment period of 60 days. The business has launched several new product ranges which will increase the inventory holding period by 9 days and because of the new mix of customers the average receivables' collection period will be 46 days. Supplier payments will be unaffected.

What is the cash operating cycle of the business before and after the planned changes?

Before	After	Tick one
145 days	40 days	
25 days	40 days	
145 days	160 days	
25 days	160 days	

Task 6.6

Select from the picklists to complete the following sentences.

Over-trading can occur when a business has [▼] working capital.

Over-capitalisation occurs when a business has [▼] working capital.

Picklist:

too little
too much

Task 6.7

(a)   A business has the following balances at the end of 20X9:

	20X9 £
Inventory	95,000
Receivables	100,000
Cash	5,000
Bank overdraft	40,000
Trade payables	80,000

What is the current ratio (to 2 decimal places)?

£ [   ]

(b)   If there is a sudden change in the current ratio and it becomes much lower than usual, what does this mean?

[▼]

Picklist:

The risk of overtrading has been reduced.
There is a risk that the business may be unable to pay its payables on time.

Task 6.8

You work for a manufacturing company that is facing a short-term liquidity problem. Which of the following assets would you recommend that it sells in order to bridge the cash deficit while doing the minimum damage to its core activities?

Explain the reasons for your decision.

1   10% of its fleet of delivery vehicles

2   Some of its plant and machinery

3   The patent on a new design

4   Its 60% equity stake in the company that supplies a scarce raw material for the manufacturing process

Task 6.9

A company has been expanding very rapidly and has now encountered a liquidity problem, as illustrated by the most recent statement of financial position reproduced below.

Statement of financial position extracts

	As at 31 December 20X2 £	As at 31 December 20X1 £
Non-current assets	350,000	270,000
Current assets:		
Inventory	200,000	95,000
Receivables	250,000	100,000
Cash	Nil	5,000
	450,000	200,000
Capital and reserves:		
Issued share capital	15,000	15,000
Reserves	355,000	335,000
Equity shareholders' funds	370,000	350,000
Current liabilities:		
Bank overdraft	200,000	40,000
Trade payables	230,000	80,000
	430,000	120,000

Other information

Sales for the year to 31 December 20X1 were £1.5m, yielding a gross profit of £300,000, and a net profit before tax of £90,000.

Sales for the year to 31 December 20X2 were £3m, with a gross profit of £450,000, and net profit before tax of £60,000.

At the beginning of the year to 31 December 20X2 the company bought new manufacturing equipment and recruited six more sales staff.

(a) Illustrating your answer with figures taken from the question, explain why it is not unusual for manufacturing companies to face a cash shortage when sales are expanding very rapidly.

(b) How have the levels of short-term and long-term debt changed between the two years, and what are the dangers of this financing position?

(c) Suggest ways in which the company might seek to resolve its current funding problems, and avoid the risks associated with overtrading.

Task 6.10

(a) **What are the three different offences related to money laundering listed in the Proceeds of Crime Act 2002? Illustrate your answer with an example of each**

(b) **Select from the picklists to complete the following sentences.**

Offering a bribe is known as [　　　　　▼] bribery.

Accepting a bribe is known as [　　　　　▼] bribery.

Picklist:

active
consensual
passive
positive

Task 6.11

Given below is the statement of profit or loss for a business for the year ending 31 March 20X9 and a statement of financial position at that date.

Statement of profit or loss

	£	£
Revenue		2,650,400
Cost of sales		
Opening inventory	180,000	
Purchases	1,654,400	
	1,834,400	
Less closing inventory	191,200	
		1,643,200
Gross profit		1,007,200
Less expenses		
Selling and distribution costs	328,400	
Administration expenses	342,200	
		670,600
Operating profit		336,600
Interest payable		36,000
Profit after interest		300,600

Statement of financial position

	£
Non-current assets	1,920,400
Current assets:	
Inventory	191,200
Receivables	399,400
Bank	16,800
	607,400
Total assets	2,527,800
Equity and liabilities:	
Equity	1,000,000
Other reserves	150,000
Retained earnings	587,500
	1,737,500
Non-current liabilities	600,000
Current liabilities:	
Payables	190,300
Total equity and liabilities	2,527,800

Using the statement of profit or loss and statement of financial position complete the table to calculate the performance indicators: Give your answer to TWO decimal places unless otherwise stated.

Return on capital employed	
Current ratio	
Quick ratio	
Receivables' collection period (to the nearest whole number)	
Inventory holding period in days (to the nearest whole number)	
Payables' payment period (to the nearest whole number)	

Task 6.12

A business has the following current asset balance and current ratio at the end of 20X9:

	20X9 £
Current assets	87,500
Current ratio	3.5

What is the current liabilities balance at the end of 20X9 (to the nearest whole number)?

£

Chapter 7 – Raising finance

Task 7.1

Are the following statements true or false? Tick the correct box.

Primary banks are those that are involved with the cheque clearing system.

	✓
True	
False	

Secondary banks are also known as commercial banks.

	✓
True	
False	

Task 7.2

A bank customer has an overdraft.

Which party is the payable (creditor)? Tick as appropriate.

	✓
Bank	
Customer	

Task 7.3

State six of a bank's main duties to its customer.

-
-
-
-
-
-

Task 7.4

Pravina, an 18-year old who lives next door to you, is about to open her first bank account.

Explain to her the rights the bank has in its relationship with her.

Task 7.5

What are the most common reasons underlying a business's need to raise additional finance?

Task 7.6

Which of the following best describe the main features of overdraft finance?

(i)   High interest rate
(ii)   Repayable in instalments
(iii)   Useful for capital expenditure
(iv)   Low interest rate
(v)   Short-term form of finance
(vi)   Repayable on demand
(vii)   Available as long as required

Tick one option

	✓
(i), (ii), (iii)	
(i), (v), (vi)	
(iii), (iv), (vii)	
(ii), (iv), (v)	

Task 7.7

Which of the following best describes the main features of a bank loan?

(i)   High interest rate
(ii)   Repayments can be negotiated
(iii)   Useful for capital expenditure
(iv)   Low interest rate
(v)   Short-term form of finance
(vi)   Repayable on demand
(vii)   Available as long as required

Tick one option

	✓
(i), (ii), (iii)	
(ii), (iv), (vi)	
(i), (v), (vii)	
(ii), (iii), (iv)	

Task 7.8

Both overdraft finance and bank loan finance have various advantages.

Complete the table by entering each of the advantages against the correct type of financing.

Type of finance	Advantages
Overdraft	▼
Bank loan	▼

Picklist:

Covenants not normally included
Precise amount required does not need to be known
Relatively low cost
Repayments can be negotiated
Security not normally required
Useful to fund capital expenditure

Task 7.9

An agricultural business has purchased a new tractor costing £63,800. It has funded the purchase with a medium-term bank loan for the full amount. The business must repay the loan over three years, with monthly payments of £2,380.

Assuming simple interest, calculate the total interest cost (to the nearest £) and the simple annual interest rate (rounded to one decimal place).

Total interest cost (£)	
Simple annual interest rate %	

Task 7.10

A business has applied for a bank loan of £22,500 to purchase some new computers for its head office. The bank requires the loan to be paid off in equal monthly instalments over two and a half years, charging simple interest at 5.25% per annum on the initial loan capital.

What are the monthly payments for the repayments of the capital and the interest on this loan? Round to the nearest pence.

Repayment of capital	
Repayment of interest	

Task 7.11

A bank charges overdraft interest at the rate of 4% per annum.

What is the appropriate interest rate if simple interest is to be applied monthly on the overdrawn balance?

Monthly interest rate (%)	

Task 7.12

A bank loan, which is to be repaid in equal monthly instalments over three years, carries a flat rate of interest of 13%.

Choose from the picklists to complete the following sentences.

The APR on the loan would be [▼]

Picklist:

higher.
lower.

Flat rate interest is charged on [▼]

Picklist:

the amount of the loan principal outstanding.
the original capital.

Task 7.13

A small private limited company requires finance for an expansion project which will require £50,000 of capital expenditure and £10,000 of additional working capital. The finance director has been investigating methods of raising this finance and has found three potential options.

Option 1   A bank loan for £60,000 secured on the non-current assets of the company. The loan is to be repaid in equal instalments over a three-year period and has a fixed rate of interest for the first year of 5%. Thereafter the rate of interest will be variable at 2.5% above the base rate. There will be an arrangement fee for the loan of 0.6% of the bank loan payable at the start of the loan term.

Option 2   The four family directors will all take out a personal secured loan of £15,000 at an annual interest rate of 4%. This money will then be loaned to the company and the personal interest cost for the directors recouped from the company.

Option 3   A bank loan for £50,000 could be taken out secured on the value of the new machinery required for the expansion. The loan will be repaid in equal instalments over five years and the interest is at a fixed rate of 5.5% based upon the outstanding capital balance at the start of the year. An arrangement fee of 0.75% of the bank loan is payable at the beginning of the loan term.

In order to fund the working capital the bank is also offering an overdraft facility of £15,000 which attracts an annual interest rate of 11%. The directors believe that they will require an average overdraft of £8,500 for just the first ten months of the year.

The Articles of Association of the company include the following in respect of the raising of finance:

- Loan finance can be secured on the assets of the company.

- The company must not accept loans from officers or directors of the company.

- The maximum overdraft allowed is £18,000.

- The interest cost to the company of any financing options should be kept as low as possible.

(a) Complete the table below to calculate the cost to the company for the first year of financing under each of the three options.

	Arrangement fee	Loan interest £	Overdraft interest £	Total cost £
Option 1				
Option 2				
Option 3				

(b) Which financial option should the company select taking account of the provisions of the Articles of Association?

Option 1	
Option 2	
Option 3	
None of the options	

Task 7.14

Famous Ltd is a quoted company which produces a range of branded products, all of which are well-established in their markets, although overall sales have grown by an average of only 2% per annum over the past decade. The board of directors is currently concerned about the company's level of financial gearing. Although the level is not high by industry standards, it is close to breaking the requirements of a loan obtained in 20W2, at a time of high market interest rates. The loan was taken out in order to finance the purchase of land and property, which was used as security for the loan. The loan is repayable in 20X7, with an option to make an early repayment from 20X4.

There are two covenants attaching to the loan, which state:

'At no time shall the ratio of debt capital to shareholders' funds exceed 50%. The company shall also maintain a prudent level of liquidity, defined as a current ratio at no time outside the range of the industry average (as published by the corporate credit analysts, Creditex), plus or minus 20%.'

Famous Ltd's most recent set of accounts is shown in summarised form below. Most of the machinery is only two or three years old, having been purchased mainly using a bank overdraft. The interest rate payable on the bank overdraft is currently 9% pa. The finance director argues that Famous Ltd should take advantage of historically low interest rates on the money markets by issuing a medium-term bond

at 5%. Famous Ltd's ordinary shares currently look unattractive compared to comparable companies in the sector which pay out higher dividends compared to the price of the shares. According to the latest published credit assessment by Creditex, the average current ratio for the industry is 1.35.

Summarised financial accounts for the year ended 30 June 20X4

Statement of financial position as at 30 June 20X4

	£m	£m
Assets employed		
Non-current (net):		
Land		5.0
Buildings		4.0
Machinery and vehicles		11.0
		20.0
Current:		
Inventory	2.5	
Trade and other receivables	4.0	
Cash	0.5	
		7.0
Total assets		27.0
Financed by:		
Ordinary shares (25p)		5.0
Reserves		10.0
Long-term payables:		
15% Loan notes 20X4-X7		5.0
Current liabilities:		
Payables	4.0	
Bank overdraft	3.0	
		7.0
Total equity and liabilities		27.0

Statement of profit or loss extracts for the year ended 30 June 20X4

	£m
Revenue	28.00
Profit from operating activities	3.00
Finance costs	(1.00)
Profit before tax	2.00
Tax expense	(0.66)
Profit for the year	1.34
Dividend	(0.70)
Retained profit	0.64

It is now December 20X4.

(a) **Explain and calculate appropriate gearing ratios for Famous Ltd.**

(b) Assess how close the company is to breaching the loan covenants.

(c) Discuss whether the gearing is in any sense 'dangerous'.

(d) Discuss what financial policies the company might adopt in order to lower its capital gearing and its interest payments.

Task 7.15

Briefly describe the main features of:

(a) **A hire purchase**
(b) **A finance lease**
(c) **An operating lease**

Task 7.16

Skint Co is a small family owned company that makes fuses for electrical plugs. It was set up twenty-five years ago by its main shareholder, Mr Holmes, who is also managing director of the company.

The company is facing short-term cash flow difficulties. It is already a highly geared company and Mr Holmes is concerned that the bank will not lend it any more money. He is considering applying for a personal loan or giving a personal guarantee in order to solve the company's short-term cash flow difficulties.

List and explain FOUR general factors that will be taken into account by a bank when deciding whether or not to lend money to a client.

Task 7.17

Fibre Clean Ltd is a small company specializing in the cleaning of carpets. Mr Sykes, the owner, is considering taking on a number of commercial clients instead of his domestic work as profit margins are higher. However, he is worried about managing the administrative workload and what the effect of providing credit will be on his cash position. He is already overdrawn.

Explain the meaning of debt factoring and invoice discounting to My Sykes, highlighting any differences between the two and suggest which one may be more useful for Mr Sykes.

Chapter 8 – Managing surplus funds

Task 8.1

Briefly explain the three main factors that should influence any decisions regarding investment of surplus funds.

Task 8.2

A business has £20,000 available to invest in a deposit for 12 months and wishes to achieve a rate of return of 4% per annum.

Which of the following investments would the business accept?

	Will accept ✓
Investment paying interest of £300 every 6 months	
Investment with a lump sum return of £800 at the end of one year	
Investment paying annual interest of £600 plus a bonus of 1% of the capital invested if the deposit is retained for 1 year	

The business is likely to be able to earn a higher rate of return if the period of time that the capital is available to invest increases.

	✓
True	
False	

If the business wants to be able to withdraw funds on demand this is likely to increase the rate of return available.

	✓
True	
False	

Task 8.3

Which of the following are true about gilt-edged securities?

(i)   They are issued by local authorities.
(ii)   They are variable rate investments.
(iii) The interest is paid twice a year.
(iv)   They are fixed rate investments.
(v)   They are issued by the government.

Tick the correct answer.

	✓
(i), (ii), (iii)	
(ii), (iii), (v)	
(iii), (iv), (v)	
(ii), (iv), (v)	

Task 8.4

Interest rates are set to fall in the near future.

What effect will this have on the price of gilt-edged securities? Tick the correct answer.

	✓
Their price will rise.	
Their price will fall.	

Task 8.5

A business has £100,000 to invest for a period of approximately six months. Investment in either a bank deposit account or gilt-edged securities is being considered.

What would be the effect of an increase in interest rates on both of these potential investments? Tick the appropriate boxes in the table below.

	Bank deposit	Gilt-edged securities
Increase in value		
Decrease in value		
No effect		

Task 8.6

A business makes a proportion of its sales for cash through a factory outlet.

What security procedures should be adopted for the safe custody of this cash?

Task 8.7

Azrina Ltd manufactures cycles. The company's long-term cash flow forecasts suggest a cash surplus of £1m will be generated in 20X7 and £1.75m in 20X8.

The company is considering its future cash management strategy and is examining four business strategies.

For each of the following four strategy scenarios, complete the table to show what action you would take to manage the cash surplus.

(a) No further growth in Azrina Ltd's existing business and no plans for further capital investment

(b) Plans for an acquisition of a cycle parts manufacturer (valued up to £5m) when a suitable opportunity arises

(c) Development in 20X7 and 20X8 of several new product lines requiring capital investment of £2.5m

(d) Phased development of two new product lines requiring capital investment of £1.25m and the intention to acquire another cycle parts manufacturer (value up to £3m) when a suitable opportunity arises

Possible action	Strategy
Invest in marketable securities	
Spend surplus cash	
Repay surplus cash to owners	
Retain cash for ease of availability	

Task 8.8

A company has produced a cash budget and believes that it will have £50,000 to invest in three months' time. The finance director has identified three possible investment options:

Option 1   Maximum investment £75,000, minimum investment £15,000. Interest rate 1.8% above base rate. 60-day notice period. Low risk and no investment in shares.

Option 2   Minimum investment of £50,000. Interest rate of 2.5%. 90-day notice period. Medium risk and no investment in shares.

Option 3   Minimum investment of £55,000. Interest rate of 3%. 30-day notice period. Low risk and no investment in shares.

The company's treasury policy for investment is as follows:

- Interest rate must be at least 2% above base rate which is currently 0.4%.
- The investment must be convertible into cash within 60 days.
- The investment must be low or medium risk.
- The investment must not include shares.

(a) **Complete the table below to show which of the policy requirements are met by each of the options.**

	Investment of £50,000	Interest 2% above base rate	Convertible within 60 days	Low/medium risk	No shares
Option 1					
Option 2					
Option 3					

(b) **Which option should be selected?**

Option 1	
Option 2	
Option 3	
None of the options	

(c) **Describe the company's appetite for risk with reference to other risk attitudes.**

Task 8.9

In the past a company has invested surplus funds in a variety of Treasury stocks and also in fixed term deposits with the bank.

(a) **Selecting from the picklists, complete the following sentences.**

Gilt-edged securities or gilts are (1) [_____ ▼] British Government securities.

They pay a (2) [_____ ▼] amount of interest and are available with varying maturity dates which is the date

(3) [_____ ▼].

Picklist:

(1) marketable/non-marketable
(2) variable/fixed/capped
(3) on which they will be redeemed/they must be kept until

(b) **If interest rates increase what effect will this have on the interest rate for gilt-edged stocks and a bank deposit account?**

Gilt-edged stocks	Bank deposit account	✓
Increase	No change	
Decrease	No change	
No change	Increase	
No change	Decrease	

(c) **If interest rates increase what effect will this have on the redemption value for gilt-edged stocks and a bank deposit account?**

Gilt-edged stocks	Bank deposit account	✓
Increase	No change	
Decrease	No change	
No change	Increase	
No change	Decrease	

Task 8.10

The following information relates to the ordinary shares of G Ltd.

Dividend per share   £0.24
Dividend yield   4.8%

What is the current price of the share?

	✓
£0.20	
£0.50	
£5.00	
£11.52	

Task 8.11

A company has forecast that it will have surplus funds to invest for a 12 month period. It is considering two investments as follows:

Investment 1

Invest in a bank deposit account that pays compound interest at a variable rate. The current rate of interest on the account is 1.1% per quarter.

Investment 2

Buy a 12 month fixed dated government bond. The bond has a simple interest rate of 2.5% payable every six months.

Explain the advantages and disadvantages to the company of each of the investments.

You should consider the return offered and the level and type of risk involved with each investment. You should assume that there are no other investments available and that these investments are only available now.

Task 8.12

Why might a company decide to have a treasury department in addition to its finance function, and what would be the main functions of this department?

Task 8.13

A company, Selfbuild Ltd, plans to construct a factory and has raised cash through an equity share issue to pay the costs. However, the building of the factory has been delayed and payments will be required three or four months later than expected. Selfbuild Ltd has decided to invest these surplus funds until they are required.

One of the directors of Selfbuild Ltd has identified three possible investment opportunities:

(i)   Treasury bills issued by the central bank. They could be purchased for a period of 91 days. The likely purchase price is £990 per £1,000.

(ii)   Equities quoted on the local stock exchange. The stock exchange has had a good record recently with the equity index increasing in value for 14 consecutive months. The director recommends investment in three large multinational companies with a history of paying an annual dividend that provides an annual yield of 10% on the current share price.

(iii)   The company's bank would pay 3.5% per year on money placed in a deposit account with 30 day's notice.

Prepare notes for the director on the risk and effective return of each of the above investment opportunities and recommend which is most suitable for Selfbuild Ltd.

Task 8.14

(a) Describe the two central roles of the Bank of England

(b) **What is the purpose of the Financial Policy Committee of the Bank of England?**

(c) **What is the purpose of the Prudential Regulatory Authority?**

Task 8.15

A company, Hillside Storage PLC, has identified it is likely to have a significant cash surplus in two months' time that is projected to last for around three months.

The treasurer has identified some corporate bonds about to be issued that meet Hillside's requirements for profitability, liquidity and security. The purpose of the bond issue is that the company intends to move its manufacturing base to a low cost location with a bad reputation for worker exploitation. Employment law is lax in this location, therefore the exploitation of employees is common.

What impact could investing the surplus funds in this way have on Hillside Storage and why?

Answer Bank

Chapter 1

Task 1.1

If a business makes a profit this means that its revenue is greater than its expenses.

Cash flow and profit will not normally be the same figure for a period.

Task 1.2

1   Accruals accounting
2   Non-cash expenses
3   Capital introduced or dividends/drawings paid
4   Purchase of non-current assets
5   Sale of non-current assets

Task 1.3

	£000
Sales receipts	820
Purchase payments	575
Overhead payments	95

Workings

Sales receipts	=	860 + 45 – 85	=	820
Purchase payments	=	600 + 75 – 100	=	575
Overhead payments	=	100 + 40 – 45	=	95

Task 1.4

The correct answer is:

	✓
£12,500	
£14,500	
£27,000	
£39,500	✓

The carrying amount of non-current assets increased by £27,000 but this was after deducting £12,500 of depreciation, so the cash paid for new assets must have been £27,000 + £12,500 = £39,500.

Task 1.5

The correct answer is:

	✓
£21,500	
£56,500	
£70,000	
£91,500	✓

The carrying amount of the building at the date of disposal is £56,500 (105,000 –48,500). If it is sold for a profit of £35,000, it must have been sold for more than its carrying amount, so the cash proceeds are £56,500 + £35000 = £91,500.

Task 1.6

Sales Ledger Control Account

	Dr £		Cr £
Opening trade receivables	34,500		
Sales revenue per statement of profit or loss	252,000	Cash received	238,600
		Closing trade receivables	47,900
	286,500		286,500

Chapter 2

Task 2.1

Week	Day	Takings £	Five-day moving average £
1	Monday	1,260	
	Tuesday	1,600	
	Wednesday	1,630	1,620
	Thursday	1,780	1,636
	Friday	1,830	1,666
2	Monday	1,340	1,668
	Tuesday	1,750	1,682
	Wednesday	1,640	1,712
	Thursday	1,850	1,754
	Friday	1,980	1,736
3	Monday	1,550	1,732
	Tuesday	1,660	1,736
	Wednesday	1,620	1,734
	Thursday	1,870	
	Friday	1,970	

Task 2.2

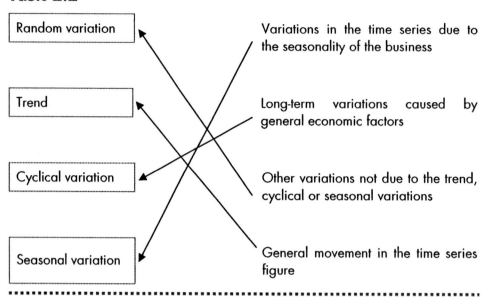

Random variation		Variations in the time series due to the seasonality of the business
Trend		Long-term variations caused by general economic factors
Cyclical variation		Other variations not due to the trend, cyclical or seasonal variations
Seasonal variation		General movement in the time series figure

Task 2.3

(a)

	Sales volume Units	Trend Units	Monthly variation (volume less trend) Units
January	20,000		
February	17,400	17,900	–500
March	16,300	18,700	–2,400
April	22,400	19,500	2,900
May	19,800	20,300	–500
June	18,700	21,100	–2,400
July	24,800	21,900	2,900
August	22,200	22,700	–500
September	21,100	23,500	–2,400
October	27,200	24,300	2,900
November	24,600	25,100	–500
December	23,500		

The monthly sales volume trend is | 800 | units.

(Working: (25,100 – 17,900)/9 changes in trend)

(b)   The variation for January is not given. However the variations can be seen to repeat and sum to zero on a quarterly basis (–500, –2400, +2900). Thus the variation for December would be –2400 and that for January +2900.

	Forecast trend Units	Variation Units	Forecast sales volume Units
January (25,100 + (2 × 800))	26,700	2,900	29,600
February (25,100 + (3 × 800))	27,500	–500	27,000
March (25,100 + (4 × 800))	28,300	–2,400	25,900

Task 2.4

Average increase in trend value $= \dfrac{(9,705 - 7,494)}{11}$

$= 201 \text{ units}$

Future trend values

Quarter 1 (9,705 + 201) = 9,906 units
Quarter 2 (9,705 + (2 × 201)) = 10,107 units
Quarter 3 (9,705 + (3 × 201)) = 10,308 units
Quarter 4 (9,705 + (4 × 201)) = 10,509 units

Quarter	Trend forecast	Average seasonal variation	Forecast of actual sales units	Forecast revenue £
1	9,906	+53	9,959	448,155
2	10,107	+997	11,104	499,680
3	10,308	+1,203	11,511	517,995
4	10,509	–2,253	8,256	371,520

Task 2.5

	£
January sales 21,000 × £30 × 60%	378,000
February sales 22,000 × £30 × 1.04 × 40%	274,560
Total March receipts	**652,560**

Task 2.6

The correct answer is:

	✓
£347,000	
£355,729	✓
£351,338	
£360,176	

March cash outflow for overheads   = £347,000 × 1.0125 × 1.0125

                                        = £355,729

Task 2.7

	£
December	2.60 × 169.0/166.3 = £2.64
January	2.60 × 173.4/166.3 = £2.71
February	2.60 × 177.2/166.3 = £2.77

Task 2.8

Forecast P12 sales = $((27 \times 12) - 24) \times 1.35 = 405$ units

Task 2.9

There are two basic approaches to sales forecasting:

(i)   Use of internal estimates

In-house sales staff can forecast future sales using their experience and knowledge and by considering the following factors:

(1)   Past sales figures
(2)   Economic environment
(3)   Competitor actions

(ii) Statistical techniques

Statistical techniques are most appropriate if past sales patterns give some indication of future sales patterns or there is correlation between two factors – that is there is a relationship between two variables.

Using historical data – a time series, and analysing these figures, the patterns and relationships can be determined and used to predict future performance.

The time series has four components:

- Trend (the general movement of the figures)

- Cyclical variation (due to general economic conditions)

- Seasonal variation (due to the time of year, month or other time period)

- Random variation (due to unpredictable events)

The techniques that can be used include regression analysis by the least squares method in combination with moving averages analysis.

Task 2.10

(a)   For time period 33, x = 33

If y = 10,000 + 4,200x, then y = 148,600

Time period 33 is a first quarter and so the seasonal variation index value is 120.

Forecast = 148,600 × 1.2 = 178,320

(b) The problems of extrapolating past performance into the future stem from the assumptions made in such extrapolations.

(i) External conditions are assumed to remain unchanged. This can make extrapolated data invalid. For example, changes in the rate of sales tax (such as VAT) may affect sales prices and so the pattern of demand in the future.

(ii) The relationship between the variables is assumed to be linear. For example, it may be assumed that if sales volume doubles then variable cost will also double. This may have been true for activity levels experienced in the past but it may not be valid to assume that the relationship will hold for activity levels in the future.

(iii) It is assumed that all variables affecting past performance have been identified and that other conditions have remained constant. The identified variables may not be the only factors affecting performance and the omission of other valid variables will affect the accuracy of the extrapolation.

These problems do not mean that the extrapolation of past performance into the future has no value. It is important that the resulting forecast is used with caution, however. Anyone relying on the forecast as the basis for decision making must be aware of its shortcomings and of any assumptions on which it is based.

Chapter 3

Task 3.1

Type of receipt/payment	Example
Regular revenue receipts	Income received from the operating activities of the business which are expected to occur frequently
Regular revenue payments	Payments due to the operating activities of the business that are expected to be incurred frequently
Exceptional receipts/payments	Income received from HM Revenue and Customs
	Income received from the operating activities of the business which are not expected to occur frequently
	Payments due to the operating activities of the business that are not expected to be incurred frequently
Capital payments/receipts	Income that arises from the proceeds of the sale of non-current assets
	Payments that arise from the acquisition of non-current assets
	Income received from the owner of the business
Drawings/dividends	Payments made to the owner of the business

Task 3.2

	October £	November £	December £
Cash sales			
October 280,000 × 30%	84,000		
November 250,000 × 30%		75,000	
December 220,000 × 30%			66,000
Credit sales			
August 240,000 × 30%	72,000		
September 265,000 × 40%	106,000		
September 265,000 × 30%		79,500	
October 280,000 × 40%		112,000	
October 280,000 × 30%			84,000
November 250,000 × 40%			100,000
Total cash receipts	**262,000**	**266,500**	**250,000**

Task 3.3

	October £	November £	December £
August 180,000 × 35%	63,000		
September 165,000 × 45%	74,250		
September 165,000 × 35%		57,750	
October 190,000 × 20% × 98%	37,240		
October 190,000 × 45%		85,500	
October 190,000 × 35%			66,500
November 200,000 × 20% × 98%		39,200	
November 200,000 × 45%			90,000
December 220,000 × 20% × 98%			43,120
Total cash payments	**174,490**	**182,450**	**199,620**

Task 3.4

	January £	February £	March £
Purchases	22,000	24,000	26,000
Cash sales = Purchases × 150%	33,000	36,000	39,000

The margin that the retailer is making is 33.33%.

(Working: January profit is £11,000 (£33,000 – £22,000), so profit margin = 11,000/33,000 = 33.33%)

Task 3.5

(a)

	April £	May £	June £
March sales 650,000 × 70%	455,000		
April sales 600,000 × 25% × 97%	145,500		
April sales 600,000 × 70%		420,000	
May sales 580,000 × 25% × 97%		140,650	
May sales 580,000 × 70%			406,000
June sales 550,000 × 25% × 97%			133,375
Total cash receipts	**600,500**	**560,650**	**539,375**

(b)

	April £	May £	June £
March sales 650,000 × 70%	455,000		
April sales 600,000 × 30% × 95%	171,000		
April sales 600,000 × 70%		420,000	
May sales 580,000 × 30% × 95%		165,300	
May sales 580,000 × 70%			406,000
June sales 550,000 × 30% × 95%			156,750
Total cash receipts	**626,000**	**585,300**	**562,750**

Task 3.6

(a) Closing receivables = 290,510/365 × 49 = £39,000

Cash received is therefore:

	£
Opening receivables	22,000
Credit sales	290,510
Closing receivables	(39,000)
Cash received	**273,510**

(b) Sales revenue for the year net of irrecoverable debts = £492,750 × 95% = £468,112.50. (Alternative approach: Irrecoverable debts for the year = 5% × £492,750 = £24,637.50. Hence sales revenue that will actually be collected in cash = £492,750 − £24,637.50 = £468,112.50)

Closing receivables at year end (net of irrecoverable debts) = £468,112.50 × 60/365 = £76,950. (Alternative calculation = £492,750 × 60/365 × 95% = £76,950)

Expected cash receipts = opening receivables + sales revenue during the year − closing receivables

= £83,000 + £468,112.50 − £76,950
= £474,162.50

Task 3.7

Month	Receipt £
January	30,100.00
February	145,569.62
March	104,166.67
April	324,000.00

Workings

NOK350,000 × £0.086 = £30,100.00
$230,000 ÷ $1.58 = £145,569.62
SFr150,000 ÷ SFr1.44 = £104,166.67
€450,000 × £0.72 = £324,000.00

Task 3.8

Labour budget – hours	May Hours	June Hours	July Hours
May 7,050/3	2,350		
June 6,450/3		2,150	
July 6,000/3			2,000
Labour budget – £	**April £**	**May £**	**June £**
April 2,350 × £8.40	19,740		
May 2,150 × £8.40		18,060	
June 2,000 × £8.40			16,800

Chapter 4

Task 4.1

(a) The correct answer is Y only.

Workings

Cost of not taking discount (and therefore taking credit from the supplier) =

$$\left(\frac{100}{100-d}\right)^{\frac{12}{m}} \text{ where } d = \% \text{ discount,}$$

m = reduction in payment period in months necessary to achieve discount

Cost of taking credit from X = $\left(\frac{100}{97}\right)^{4} - 1 = 12.96\%$

Cost of taking credit from Y = $\left(\frac{100}{96}\right)^{3} - 1 = 13.02\%$

Thus it is cheaper to use the overdraft at a cost of 13% to fund immediate payment to Y, whereas it is better to take credit from X for three months.

(Note that the formula here uses months because this is how the settlement period is expressed but can be changed if the settlement terms are expressed in days – see below.)

(b) Cost of early settlement discount is estimated using the formula

$$= \left(\frac{100}{100-d}\right)^{\frac{365}{t}} - 1$$

$$= \left(\frac{100}{100-2.5}\right)^{\frac{365}{65-15}} - 1$$

$$= \left(\frac{100}{97.5}\right)^{7.3} - 1$$

$$= 20.3\%$$

(c) Evaluation of change in credit policy

Current average collection period	= 40 days
Current accounts receivable	= £4m × 40/365
	= £438,356
Average collection period under new policy	= (25% × 10 days) + (75% × 50 days)
	= 40 days

New level of credit sales	$= £4m \times 1.08$
	$= £4.32m$
Accounts receivable after policy change	$= £4.32m \times 40/365$
	$= £473,425$
Increase in financing cost	$= £(473,425 - 438,356) \times 5\%$
	$= £1,753$

	£
Increase in financing cost	1,753
Incremental costs (£4.32m × 1%)	43,200
Sales revenue foregone due to discount (25% × £4.32m × 2%)	21,600
Increase in costs	66,553
Contribution from increased sales (£4m × 8% × 50%)	160,000
Net benefit of policy change	93,447

The proposed policy will therefore increase profitability.

Task 4.2

(a) Purchases budget

	April kgs	May kgs	June kgs	July kgs
Materials required for production				
April 1,220 × 2 kg	2,440			
May 1,320 × 2 kg		2,640		
June 1,520 × 2 kg			3,040	
July 1,620 × 2 kg				3,240
Opening inventory	–550	–500	–450	–400
Closing inventory	500	450	400	350
Purchases in kgs	2,390	2,590	2,990	3,190

	April £	May £	June £	July £
April 2,390 × £40	95,600			
May 2,590 × £40		103,600		
June 2,990 × £40			119,600	
July 3,190 × £40				127,600

(b) Cash payments to suppliers for May to July

	May £	June £	July £
Cash payments	95,600	103,600	119,600

Task 4.3

(a) Cash receipts from customers

	Workings	July £	August £	September £
April sales	420,000 × 12%	50,400		
May sales	400,000 × 25%	100,000		
	400,000 × 12%		48,000	
June sales	480,000 × 40%	192,000		
	480,000 × 25%		120,000	
	480,000 × 12%			57,600
July sales	500,000 × 20% × 96%	96,000		
	500,000 × 40%		200,000	
	500,000 × 25%			125,000
August sales	520,000 × 20% × 96%		99,840	
	520,000 × 40%			208,000
September sales	510,000 × 20% × 96%			97,920
Total receipts		**438,400**	**467,840**	**488,520**

(b) Cash payments to suppliers

	Workings	July £	August £	September £
May purchases	250,000 × 60%	150,000		
June purchases	240,000 × 40%	96,000		
	240,000 × 60%		144,000	
July purchases	280,000 × 40%		112,000	
	280,000 × 60%			168,000
August purchases	300,000 × 40%			120,000
Total payments		**246,000**	**256,000**	**288,000**

(c) Cash payments for general overheads

	Workings	July £	August £	September £
June overheads	(50,000 – 6,000) × 25%	11,000		
July overheads	(50,000 – 6,000) × 75%	33,000		
	(50,000 – 6,000) × 25%		11,000	
August overheads	(55,000 – 6,000) × 75%		36,750	
	(55,000 – 6,000) × 25%			12,250
September overheads	(55,000 – 6,000) × 75%			36,750
Total overhead payments		**44,000**	**47,750**	**49,000**

(d) Cash budget – July to September

	July £	August £	September £
Receipts			
Receipts from credit sales	438,400	467,840	488,520
Proceeds from sale of equipment	0	7,500	0
Total receipts	**438,400**	**475,340**	**488,520**
Payments			
Payments to suppliers	–246,000	–256,000	–288,000
Wages	–60,000	–60,000	–60,000
Overheads	–44,000	–47,750	–49,000
Selling expenses	–48,000	–50,000	–52,000
Equipment	0	–42,000	0
Overdraft interest	–820	–424	–233
Total payments	**–398,820**	**–456,174**	**–449,233**
Net cash flow	39,580	19,166	39,287
Opening balance	–82,000	–42,420	–23,254
Closing balance	**–42,420**	**–23,254**	**16,033**

Task 4.4

(a) Cash receipts from sales

	Workings	October £	November £	December £
August sales	5,000 × £75 × 60%	225,000		
September sales	5,100 × £75 × 40%	153,000		
	5,100 × £75 × 60%		229,500	
October sales	5,400 × £75 × 40%		162,000	
	5,400 × £75 × 60%			243,000
November sales	5,800 × £75 × 40%			174,000
Total cash receipts		**378,000**	**391,500**	**417,000**

(b) Purchases budget

	August kg	September kg	October kg	November kg
Kgs required for production Production × 3 kg	15,300	16,500	17,700	18,300
Opening inventory	–3,000	–3,000	–3,000	–3,200
Closing inventory	3,000	3,000	3,200	3,500
Purchases in kgs	**15,300**	**16,500**	**17,900**	**18,600**
	£	£	£	£
Purchases in £ Kgs × £9	**137,700**	**148,500**	**161,100**	**167,400**

(c) Payments to suppliers

		October £	November £	December £
August purchases	137,700 × 40%	55,080		
September purchases	148,500 × 60%	89,100		
	148,500 × 40%		59,400	
October purchases	161,100 × 60%		96,660	
	161,100 × 40%			64,440
November purchases	167,400 × 60%			100,440
Total cash payments		**144,180**	**156,060**	**164,880**

(d) Labour budget

	October Hours	November Hours	December Hours
Production × 3 hours	16,500	17,700	18,300
	£	£	£
Production hours × £7.20	118,800	127,440	131,760

(e) Cash budget – October to December

	October £	November £	December £
Receipts			
From credit customers	**378,000**	**391,500**	**417,000**
Payments			
To credit suppliers	–144,180	–156,060	–164,880
Wages	–118,800	–127,440	–131,760
Production overheads	–50,000	–50,000	–50,000
General overheads	–60,000	–60,000	–68,000
Total payments	**–372,980**	**–393,500**	**–414,640**
Net cash flow	5,020	–2,000	2,360
Opening bank balance	40,000	45,020	43,020
Closing bank balance	**45,020**	**43,020**	**45,380**

Task 4.5

(a) Payments to suppliers with no settlement discount

	Workings	October £	November £	December £
August purchases	520,000 × 40%	208,000		
September purchases	550,000 × 60%	330,000		
	550,000 × 40%		220,000	
October purchases	560,000 × 60%		336,000	
	560,000 × 40%			224,000
November purchases	580,000 × 60%			348,000
Total cash payments		**538,000**	**556,000**	**572,000**

(b) Payments to suppliers with settlement discount

	Workings	October £	November £	December £
August purchases	520,000 × 40%	208,000		
September purchases	550,000 × 60%	330,000		
	550,000 × 40%		220,000	
October purchases	560,000 × 30% × 97%	162,960		
	560,000 × 40%		224,000	
	560,000 × 30%			168,000
November purchases	580,000 × 30% × 97%		168,780	
	580,000 × 40%			232,000
December purchases	600,000 × 30% × 97%			174,600
Total cash payments		**700,960**	**612,780**	**574,600**

Task 4.6

(a)

	April £	May £	June £
Original value of forecast sales (£1 per unit)	140,000	150,000	155,000
Original timing of receipts	140,000	176,000	144,000
Revised value of forecast sales (£0.90 per unit)	126,000	135,000	139,500
Revised timing of receipts	140,000	170,400	129,600
Increase/(decrease) in sales receipts	**0**	**(5,600)**	**(14,400)**

Working

Original timing of receipts

May   120,000 + (40% × 140,000) = 176,000
June   (60% × 140,000) + (40% × 150,000) = 144,000

Revised timing of receipts

May   120,000 + (40% × 126,000) = 170,400
June   (60% × 126,000) + (40% × 135,000) = 129,600

(b)

	April £	May £	June £
Original net cash flow	−12,000	40,000	44,000
Increase/(decrease) in sales receipts per (a)	0	−5,600	−14,400
Revised net cash flow	−12,000	34,400	29,600
Opening bank balance	−20,000	−32,000	2,400
Closing bank balance	−32,000	2,400	32,000

Task 4.7

(a) The basic approach of sensitivity analysis is to calculate the outcomes under alternative assumptions to determine how sensitive the company's plans are to changing conditions. In the context of a cash budget, the cash flows will change if the assumptions used to formulate the budget are altered.

One approach is to develop a range of possibilities under different assumptions (eg what if the sales price is discounted by 2%, 5%, 10% respectively) and use this to prepare alternative cash budgets. Another is to measure how sensitive the budget is to changes in certain variables by calculating the impact of a particular change and comparing the original and revised cash flows. Sensitivity analysis can thus be used to assess which assumptions have the biggest impact on the budget.

It is also important to recognise that changes in one assumption may affect other variables. Here, a discount in the sales price, which by itself would have a negative impact on cash receipts may encourage more customers and hence give rise to an overall increase in sales volumes.

(b) Contribution = £3.00 – £1.65 = £1.35

(i) Sensitivity to sales volume

For profit of zero, contribution has to decrease by £7,000. This represents a reduction in sales of £7,000/(20,000 units × £1.35) = 25.93%

(ii) Sensitivity to sales price

For a profit of zero, contribution has to decrease by £7,000. This represents a reduction in selling price of 7,000/(20,000 × £3.00) = 11.67%

(iii) Sensitivity to variable costs

For a profit of zero, contribution has to decrease by £7,000. This represents an increase in variable costs of 7,000/(20,000 × £1.65) = 21.21%

Task 4.8

Output tax = £2,125,000 × 20% = £425,000
Input tax = £1,975,000 × 20% = £395,000

Amount due to HMRC = output tax less input tax = £425,000 – £395,000 = £30,000

Task 4.9

	Period 1 £000	Period 2 £000
Sales receipts (W1)	5,144	5,314
Raw materials purchases (W2)	(2,139)	(2,201)
Production wages (W3)	(1,720)	(1,722)
Variable production expenses (production units × £1.10)	(231)	(231)
Variable selling expenses (sales units × £1.60)	(240)	(320)
Fixed production expenses (W4)	(1,376)	0
Interest (W5)	0	(450)
Net cash flow for the period	(562)	390
Opening cash balance	76	(486)
Closing cash balance	(486)	(96)

Workings

1 *Sales*

	Period 1 £000	Period 2 £000
Sales (150,000 × £30 and 200,000 × £30)	4,500	6,000
Irrecoverable debts @ 2%	(90)	(120)
Net sales	4,410	5,880
Opening trade receivables	2,430	1,696
Closing trade receivables*	(1,696)	(2,262)
Receipts	5,144	5,314

* Net sales × 5/13 = 1,696

2   *Materials*

	Period 1 £000	Period 2 £000
Production (210,000 × £9.50)	1,995	1,995
Closing inventory	921*	1,125*
Opening inventory	(710)	(921)
Purchases	2,206	2,199
Opening payables	612	679
Closing payables	(679)**	(677)**
Paid	2,139	2,201

* 1,995 × 6/13 (Period 1) and 220 × £9.50 × 7/13 (Period 2)
** 2,206 × 4/13 (Period 1) and 2,199 × 4/13 (Period 2)

3   *Production wages*

	Period 1 £000	Period 2 £000
Production (210 × £8.20/unit)	1,722	1,722
Opening unpaid wages	130	132
Closing unpaid wages (£1,722/13)	(132)	(132)
Paid	1,720	1,722

4   Other fixed production expenses = 860,000 units × £3.20 = £2,752,000

Paid in period 1 = £2,752,000/2 = £1,376,000

Note. Ignore depreciation as it is a non-cash expense.

5   Annual interest = £10,000,000 × 9% = £900,000.

Paid in period 2 = £900,000/2 = £450,000

Chapter 5

Task 5.1

	Budget £	Actual £	Variance £	Adv/Fav £
Receipts:				
Cash sales receipts	101,000	94,000	7,000	Adv
Credit sales receipts	487,000	475,000	12,000	Adv
Total receipts	588,000	569,000	19,000	Adv
Payments:				
Credit suppliers	303,000	294,000	9,000	Fav
Wages	155,000	162,000	7,000	Adv
Variable overheads	98,600	99,400	800	Adv
Fixed overheads	40,000	40,000	0	
Capital expenditure	0	45,000	45,000	Adv
Total payments	596,600	640,400	43,800	Adv
Net cash flow	– 8,600	– 71,400	62,800	Adv
Balance b/f	20,300	20,300	0	
Balance c/f	11,700	– 51,100	62,800	Adv

Task 5.2

(a)

	£
Budgeted closing bank balance	61,900
Surplus in cash sales	13,000
Shortfall in credit sales receipts	–25,000
Increase in proceeds from sales from non-current assets	22,000
Increase in payments to credit suppliers	–35,000
No change in wages	0
Increase in variable overheads	–7,400
Increase in fixed overheads	–2,000
Increase in purchase of non-current assets	–46,000
No change in dividend payments	0
Actual closing bank balance	–18,500

(b)

	✓
Delay capital expenditure	
Chase customers to pay sooner	
Delay payments to suppliers	✓
Marketing campaign to increase sales	

Although the other options may have resulted in a lower overdraft it is unlikely that any of these on their own are sufficient to reduce the deficit by £18,500.

Task 5.3

(a)

	Budget February £	Actual February £	Variance £
Cash receipts			
Receipts from sales	148,800	145,600	-3,200
Deposit account interest	100	100	–
Total cash receipts	**148,900**	**145,700**	**-3,200**
Cash payments			
Payments to suppliers	-41,600	-56,000	-14,400
Salaries	-43,000	-45,150	-2,150
Administration overheads	-30,000	-30,000	–
Capital expenditure	-20,000	-6,000	+14,000
Total payments	**-134,600**	**-137,150**	**-2,550**
Net cash flow	**14,300**	**8,550**	**-5,750**
Opening cash balance	-25,900	-25,900	–
Closing cash balance	**-11,600**	**-17,350**	**-5,750**

(b)

	£
Budgeted closing bank balance	-11,600
Shortfall in sales receipts	-3,200
No change in deposit account interest	0
Increase in payments to credit suppliers	-14,400
Increase in salaries	-2,150
No change in administration overheads	0
Decrease in capital expenditure	+14,000
Actual closing bank balance	-17,350

(c)

Sales receipts	Loss of customers

Payments to suppliers	Increase in suppliers prices

Salaries	Bonus paid to staff

Capital expenditure	Negotiated credit with supplier of equipment, provided initial deposit paid in month of purchase

Task 5.4

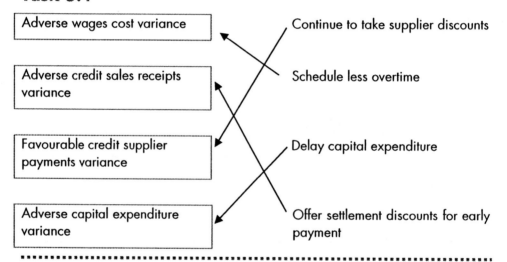

Adverse wages cost variance — Continue to take supplier discounts

Adverse credit sales receipts variance — Schedule less overtime

Favourable credit supplier payments variance — Delay capital expenditure

Adverse capital expenditure variance — Offer settlement discounts for early payment

Task 5.5

(a)

£	26,300

Budgeted overhead = £27,500 – 1,200 = £26,300

(b)

£	20,300

Budgeted cost of non-current asset = £18,000 + £2,300 = £20,300

Task 5.6

(a)

	Budget	Actual	Variance	Adv/Fav
Sales (units)	72,000	64,000	8,000	Adv
Cash received	£720,000	£430,080	289,920	Adv
Selling price	£10 per unit	£8.40 per unit	1.60	Adv

(b) Possible causes of variances:

(i) Stronger than anticipated **competition** forced prices down.

(ii) A **reduction** in the overall levels of **demand** resulted in a reduction in sales volume and a downward pressure on prices.

(iii) Cash received is lower than the sales revenue (64,000 units × £8.40 = £537,600), which indicates that not all the money was received from the sales. Strong competition may have lead to the company offering credit terms to customers, which was not budgeted for.

(iv) Poor planning techniques may have meant that the original budget was not realistic.

(c) Analysing the variances will assist the company do the following:

Improve future planning – Any non-controllable variances will need to be factored in to future plans so that the company can make decisions based on sound financial information.

Control performance – If the reasons for the variances are controllable then the company can make changes to come in on budget in future periods.

Performance management – The management of resources is a key indication of performance and so variances can be used as one method of assessing the performance of managers.

(d) Factors to be considered before deciding to investigate a variance.

Size of variance – Small variations in a single period are bound to occur and are unlikely to be significant. Obtaining an 'explanation' is likely to be time-consuming and irritating for the manager concerned. The explanation will often be 'chance', which is not, in any case, particularly helpful. For such variations further investigation is not worthwhile.

Controllability – Controllability must also influence the decision whether to investigate further. If there is a general worldwide price increase in the price of an important raw material there is nothing that can be done internally to control the effect of this. Uncontrollable variances call for a change in the plan, not an investigation into the past.

BPP
LEARNING MEDIA

Variance trend – Caution should be exercised before investigating a 'snapshot' variance in too much detail. For example, an adverse variance in Month 1 could indicate that control action is needed, but in a large company with many processes to monitor, it may be advisable to postpone direct action until the variances for subsequent months have been analysed. If they show a favourable trend then intervention will not be necessary.

You only need to discuss three factors but your answer may also have included the following.

Cost – The likely cost of an investigation needs to be weighed against the cost to the organisation of allowing the variance to continue in future periods.

Interrelationship of variances – Quite possibly, individual variances should not be looked at in isolation. One variance might be inter-related with another, and much of it might have occurred only because the other, inter-related, variance occurred too. When two variances are interdependent (interrelated) one will usually be adverse and the other one favourable.

Task 5.7

Variance analysis compares the actual effects of a business' operations to those that were anticipated in the business plans.

The business environment

Variance analysis assumes that the future is predictable. The current business environment is more dynamic and liable to change than it was in the past, so the use of variance analysis for planning and control purposes is not always ideal.

Non financial targets

Variance analysis concentrates on a **narrow range of costs** only and does not give sufficient attention to non-financial issues such as quality and customer satisfaction. For example, an aggressive credit control approach could result in a good cash flow position, but negatively impact customer goodwill and repeat sales.

Responsibility for variances

Standard costing systems make **individual managers responsible** for the variances relating to their part of the organisation's activities. Modern manufacturing techniques aim to make **all personnel** aware of, and responsible for, the importance of supplying the customer with a quality product.

Despite the arguments set out above, standard costing and variance analysis can be relevant in the modern manufacturing environment for the following reasons.

Planning. Even in a dynamic environment, budgets will still need to be quantified. The organisation needs to know what cash flow it expects in order to make enough working capital available to cover the immediate costs of the business.

Control. Changes from plan will still be relevant to performance management. Cash is a vital element of any business and therefore it is an important management role to compare the actual cash flows for a period to the expected cash flows as shown in the cash flow forecast. Variance analysis can be to used for example to identify and control trade receivables from increasing, or prevent trade payables being paid too quickly.

Task 5.8

The notes below cover a range of possible points that you may include in your written response. These examples are not intended to be exhaustive and other valid comments may be relevant.

Cash sales

- The cash sales from exams have increased by £480,000 and this equates to a favourable variance of 12.00%.

- The cash sales have increased because there has been a price increase from £45 to £50 and this has not been budgeted for.

- Increase in sales volumes.

- Possible timing difference, the volume might reduce in future months.

- Inaccurate forecasting

- The remedy would be to amend future budgets taking into account price increase.

Investment income

- Receipts from investment income are £9,000 above budget and this equates to a favourable variance of 15%.

- This is due to an increase in the bank base rate from 1.25% to 1.75% which has affected the rate of interest of the investment.

- Inaccurate forecasting. The remedy would be to amend future budgets until the rate changes again.

- Research other investments for a better return

Wages and salaries

- Wages and salaries are overspent by £230,000 and this equates to an adverse variance of 20%.

- This is due to the new exam questions being written.

- Inaccurate forecasting

- The remedy would be to increase the budget if the contingent labour workforce is still in place.

Chapter 6

Task 6.1

The cash operating cycle time is the	inventory holding period plus trade receivables' collection period less trade payables' payment period.

Liquid assets include	cash and short-term investments.

Task 6.2

The correct answer is:

	✓
1 month	
2 months	
3 months	
4 months	✓

	Months
Raw material inventory holding period	4.0
Less credit taken from suppliers	(3.0)
Finished goods inventory holding period	1.0
Trade receivables' collection period	2.0
Cash operating cycle	4.0

Task 6.3

The correct answer is:

	✓
31 days	
36 days	
46 days	
51 days	✓

Working

	Days
Inventory holding period	51
Trade receivables' collection period	77
	128
Less trade payables' payment period	(41)
Cash operating cycle	87

Task 6.4

The correct answer is:

	✓
Taking advantage of early settlement discounts offered by suppliers	
Offering an early settlement discount to customers	✓
Increasing the cash balance held in the business's current account	
Increasing the credit terms offered to customers from 30 days to 60 days	

Offering an early settlement discount to customers will hopefully encourage customers to pay earlier. This will have the effect of reducing the trade receivables' collection period, which will in turn reduce the cash operating cycle of the business.

Task 6.5

The correct answer is:

25 days	40 days	✓

Working

	Before	After
Inventory holding period	45	54
Trade receivables' collection period	40	46
Trade payables' payment period	60	60
Cash operating cycle	45 + 40 – 60 = 25	54 + 46 – 60 = 40

Task 6.6

Over-trading can occur when a business has [too little] working capital.

Over-capitalisation occurs when a business has [too much] working capital.

Task 6.7

(a) Current assets = £95,000 + £100,000 + £5,000 = £200,000

Current liabilities = £40,000 + £80,000 = £120,000

Current ratio = current assets / current liabilities

Current ratio = £200,000 / £120,000 = 1.67

(b) There is a risk that the business may be unable to pay its payables on time.

A symptom of overtrading is a reduction in the current ratio.

Quick ratio = current assets – inventory / current liabilities

Current ratio = £105,000 / £120,000 = 0.88

Task 6.8

The company should sell 10% of its delivery vehicles. It will keep the majority of its delivery vehicles, and it is safe to assume that reasonably priced alternatives are available. This sale should not damage the long term profitability of the company.

Assuming that the plant and machinery is in use and not redundant, selling this would impact a core activity of the business. In addition the likely sale proceeds may not reflect the actual value in use to the business. The plant should not be sold in these circumstances.

The patent is likely to be a key to securing the long-term future profitability of the company. It should not be sold to meet short-term needs as this will damage the company's competitive advantage.

A 60% stake constitutes a controlling interest in the supplier. Given that this supplier provides a scarce raw material to the company, selling this shareholding could damage the supply of this raw material.

Task 6.9

(a) Manufacturing companies generally have a relatively long operating cycle and a correspondingly large working capital requirement. When the level of sales increases, there is an increased investment in:

(i) Inventory, as additional raw materials are purchased to produce the additional goods.

(ii)   Staff costs, both direct in production, and indirect in sales and credit control overhead.

(iii)   Receivables since most manufacturing companies sell on credit, and additional sales will therefore translate into a higher level of receivables.

Need for working capital investment

The company may also need to purchase equipment to increase its capacity. All of these areas require an immediate investment of cash, in advance of the cash flow benefits of the additional sales and operating profits being felt. Although the company may also benefit from an increased level of payables, this will not be enough to offset the other factors, and therefore additional cash will be required to finance this process.

This problem can be illustrated using the figures from the company.

(i)   During the last year, sales have doubled by from £1.5m to £3m.

(ii)   There has been additional net investment of £80,000 in non-current assets during the same period.

(iii)   The level of inventory has more than doubled from £95,000 to £200,000.

(iv)   Receivables have increased by £150,000 from £100,000 to £250,000, an increase of 150%.

(v)   Six additional sales staff have been recruited.

These changes have resulted in a massive increase in the bank overdraft of £160,000 from £40,000 to £200,000, (£165,000 if the £5,000 cash balance in 20X1 is included) and in the level of trade payables, which has nearly trebled from £80,000 to £230,000.

The cash resources at the start of the year were only £5,000, and the increased level of trading has been financed entirely from short-term bank borrowings and trade payables.

(b) Increase in debt levels

It has been seen that there has been a large increase in the level of short-term borrowings in the form of bank loans and trade payables. The ratio of equity: bank debt has fallen from 8.75 times (£350,000/£40,000) to 1.85 times (£370,000/£200,000), and the real level of reliance on debt is even higher if the increase in the level of trade payables is taken into account. The company has financed its expansion wholly by using short-term debt.

Dangers of financing position

(i) Lack of matching

The company should match long-term assets with long-term funds. At present, both the increase in working capital and the increase in non-current assets are being financed out of short-term debt.

(ii) Exceeding terms of trade

Although the use of trade payables as a source of finance is attractive because there is rarely any interest charge, it is likely that the company is exceeding its terms of trade, since the increase in the level of payables is so much greater than the increase in the level of sales. It is therefore running the risk of losing the goodwill of its suppliers.

(iii) Inability to obtain credit

The current state of the funding means that, on the basis of the statement of financial position, the company may find it hard to obtain additional credit from existing or new suppliers. This is because of the high level of financial risk now being carried by the trade payables who have no security for their credit.

(iv) Problems with bank

There is no information on the nature of any agreements that the company has with the bank over funding, or any indication as to the size of the overdraft limit. However, as the level of short-term funding increases, the bank will want to review the current and forecast trading situation with the company before increasing its stake in the company any further. It would be in the interest of both parties if the existing overdraft were replaced with some form of secured medium-term bank debt.

(c) The main needs of the company are to reduce its reliance on short-term debt and to ease its current cash shortage. This could be achieved in the following ways.

(i) Conversion of loan

The short-term bank loan could be converted to a longer-term loan or debenture.

(ii) Increase equity

The company could seek to increase the level of equity investment, which would reduce the level of gearing to a safer level.

(iii) Improved inventory and receivable control

As has already been shown, certain elements of working capital have increased at a faster rate than the sales growth would appear to warrant. In

particular, there appears to be scope for improving the control of inventory and receivables. If both these elements were restricted in line with the growth in sales, this would release working capital. This would reduce the need for additional external funding.

Task 6.10

(a) The three specific offences noted in relation to money laundering are:

- Hiding the proceeds of crime or moving it overseas. For example, transferring funds obtained illegally to an offshore location to avoid detection.

- Allowing access to criminal property to others. For example, sharing bank account details and passwords with others so they can access the proceeds of crime.

- Acquiring property known or suspected to represent the proceeds of crime. For example, purchasing goods you know or suspect are stolen or were originally acquired by the seller using money obtained through illegal means.

(b) Offering a bribe is known as [active] bribery.

Accepting a bribe is known as [passive] bribery.

Task 6.11

Return on capital employed	14.40%
Current ratio	3.19
Quick ratio	2.19
Receivables' collection period	55 days
Inventory holding period in days	41 days
Payables' payment period	42 days

Workings

(i) Return on capital employed $= \dfrac{\text{Operating profit}}{\text{Non-current assets} + \text{Net current assets}} \times 100$

$= \dfrac{336,600}{2,337,500} \times 100$

$= 14.40\%$

(ii)   Current ratio $= \dfrac{\text{Current assets}}{\text{Current liabilities}}$

$= \dfrac{607,400}{190,300}$

$= 3.19$

(iii) Quick ratio $= \dfrac{\text{Current assets} - \text{Inventory}}{\text{Current liabilities}}$

$= \dfrac{607,400 - 191,200}{190,300}$

$= 2.19$

(iv) Receivables' collection period $= \dfrac{\text{Receivables}}{\text{Revenue}} \times 365$

$= \dfrac{399,400}{2,650,400} \times 365$

$= 55 \text{ days}$

(v)   Inventory days $= \dfrac{\text{Average inventory}}{\text{Cost of sales}} \times 365$

$= \dfrac{(180,000 + 191,200) / 2}{1,643,200} \times 365$

$= 41 \text{ days}$

(vi) Payables' payment period $= \dfrac{\text{Payables}}{\text{Purchases}} \times 365$

$= \dfrac{190,300}{1,654,400} \times 365$

$= 42 \text{ days}$

Task 6.12

£25,000

Current ratio $= \dfrac{\text{Current assets}}{\text{Current liabilities}}$

3.5 $= \dfrac{87,500}{\text{Current liabilities}}$

Therefore current liabilities $= \dfrac{87,500}{3.5}$

$= £25,000$

Chapter 7

Task 7.1

Primary banks are those that are involved with the cheque clearing system.

	✓
True	✓
False	

Secondary banks are also known as commercial banks.

	✓
True	
False	✓

Task 7.2

	✓
Bank	✓
Customer	

Task 7.3

A bank's main duties to its customers are:

- It must honour a customer's cheque provided that it is correctly made out, there is no legal reason for not honouring it and the customer has enough funds or overdraft limit to cover the amount of the cheque.

- The bank must credit cash/cheques that are paid into the customer's account.

- If the customer makes a written request for repayment of funds in their account, for example by writing a cheque, the bank must repay the amount on demand.

- The bank must comply with the customer's instructions given by direct debit mandate or standing order.

- The bank must provide a statement showing the transactions on the account within a reasonable period and provide details of the balance on the customer's account.

- The bank must respect the confidentiality of the customer's affairs unless the bank is required by law, public duty or its own interest to disclose details or where the customer gives their consent for such disclosure.

- The bank must tell the customer if there has been an attempt to forge the customer's signature on a cheque.

- The bank should use care and skill in its actions.

- The bank must provide reasonable notice if it is to close a customer's account.

Note. Only six points were required.

Task 7.4

Use of money

You cannot restrict the ways in which the bank uses your money; the money can be used in any ways that are **legally and morally acceptable**. However, the bank must make the money available to you according to the terms of your deposit; if you are opening a current account it must be **available on demand**.

Overdrawn balances

If your account shows a negative or debit balance (an **overdraft**), the bank has the right to be repaid this balance on demand. The only exception is if the bank has granted you an **overdraft facility**, which requires the bank to give you a period of notice if it wishes you to pay back what you owe it.

Charges and commissions

The bank can charge you **interest** on overdrawn balances, and can also levy **other charges and commissions** for use of its services. Depending on the terms of your account, this can even include charges for drawing cheques from your account, and withdrawing money from cashpoint machines.

Duty of care

You owe the bank a duty of care, particularly when **drawing cheques**. You should not issue cheques that are signed but lack other details such as payee or amount, nor should you write cheques out in pencil as they can easily be altered.

You should also **take care of cards** that the bank issues to you (credit, debit and cashpoint cards) and keep your **PIN number** (the number that you need to enter to use the bank's cashpoint machines) secure.

Task 7.5

The most common reasons for a business need to raise additional finance are to:

- Fund day-to-day working capital
- Increase working capital
- Reduce payables
- Purchase non-current assets
- Acquire another business

Task 7.6

The correct answer is

	✓
(i), (ii), (iii)	
(i), (v), (vi)	✓
(iii), (iv), (vii)	
(ii), (iv), (v)	

Task 7.7

The correct answer is (ii), (iii), (iv)

	✓
(i), (ii), (iii)	
(ii), (iv), (vi)	
(i), (v), (vii)	
(ii), (iii), (iv)	✓

Task 7.8

Type of finance	Advantages
Overdraft	Relatively low cost Precise amount required does not need to be known Security not normally required Covenants not normally included
Bank loan	Useful to fund capital expenditure Repayments can be negotiated

Task 7.9

Total interest cost (£)	£21,880
Simple annual interest rate %	11.4

Total repayments will be 36 × £2,380 = £85,680.

If the business has borrowed £63,800 to buy the tractor, the total interest cost is 85,680 – 63,800 = £21,880.

Over the three years of the loan, the total interest is 21,880/63,800 = 34.3%. This is equivalent to 11.4% simple interest per annum.

Task 7.10

Repayment of capital	£750
Repayment of interest	£98.44

Repayment of capital = 22,500/30 = £750 per month

Repayment of interest = (22,500 × 5.25%)/12 = £98.44

Task 7.11

Monthly interest rate (%)	0.33%

(**Working:** 4% × 1/12 = 0.33%)

Task 7.12

The APR on the loan would be [higher.]

Flat rate interest is charged on [the original capital.]

Task 7.13

(a)

	Arrangement fee £	Loan interest £	Overdraft interest £	Total cost £
Option 1	360	3,000		3,360
Option 2		2,400		2,400
Option 3	375	2,750	779	3,904

Note. Overdraft interest is calculated as £8,500 × 11% × $^{10}/_{12}$ = £779

(b)

Option 1	✓
Option 2	
Option 3	
None of the options	

Task 7.14

(a) Capital gearing

Capital gearing is concerned with a company's **long-term capital structure**. The covenant attaching to the loan does not define clearly what is meant by capital gearing in this context, in particular whether the bank overdraft should be included as part of 'debt capital'. However, since it appears that the overdraft has been used principally to finance non-current assets in the form of machinery rather than as a source of working capital, it is probably reasonable to argue that it should be included as part of the prior charge capital. The gearing ratio can thus be defined as:

$$\frac{\text{Prior charge capital}}{\text{Shareholders' funds (equity)}} = \frac{\text{Debentures + overdraft}}{\text{Ordinary shares + reserves}}$$

The gearing ratio can now be calculated. $\dfrac{£5.0m + £3.0m}{£5.0 + £10.0m} = 53.3\%$

If the overdraft is ignored, the gearing ratio would be $\dfrac{£5.0m}{£5.0 + £10.0m} = 33.3\%$

(b) Terms of covenant

It appears from the calculation in part (a) that unless the overdraft is excluded, the company has already breached the covenant relating to the gearing level which states that 'At no time shall the ratio of debt capital to shareholders' funds exceed 50%'.

If short-term payables were included, the gearing would be increased.

The required liquidity range for the current ratio is 1.08 (1.35 × 80%) to 1.62 (1.35 × 120%). The current ratio (current assets: current liabilities) for Famous Ltd is 1.0 (£7.0m:£7.0m). The company is therefore in breach of the covenant with respect to liquidity.

(c) Dangers of high gearing

A **high gearing level** only constitutes a danger if the company is at risk of being unable to meet payments (including interest on the debt) as they fall due. If this situation arises the company could be forced to **liquidate assets** to meet the demands of its payables, and this in turn could jeopardise its operating viability. It follows that the absolute level of gearing cannot be used to assess the financial risk faced by the company. It is more helpful to assess the level of interest cover in the light of pattern of income and cash inflows. The company appears to have a stable business and pattern of income that allows it to meet its payables demands.

Quality of asset backing

A further factor to take into account is the **quality of the asset backing** since this will influence the attitude of its lenders if the company faces problems in repaying its debt. Land and buildings currently appear in the accounts at £9.0m, which represent 75% of the value of total payables (including trade payables). While it is unlikely that anything close to the book valuation of plant and machinery and inventory could be realised in the event of a forced sale, it is to be hoped that the major part of the receivables figures is collectable. Therefore, the company appears to have adequate asset backing in the event of a forced restructuring or liquidation.

Conclusion

The factors discussed above, when taken together, suggest that the **level of gearing** is not particularly dangerous. However, if the company is actually in breach of its loan covenants, the courses of action available to the lender and their attitude towards the situation will be of key importance in determining the true dangers of the company's position.

(d) ## Lower Gearing

Operating leases

If the company is to lower its capital gearing it needs either to increase the value of its issued share capital and reserves or to decrease the size of its borrowings. Since growth is low and cash resources relatively small it seems unlikely the company will be able to repay much of the debt in the short-term future from operational funds. However, one option might be to convert some of the owned plant and vehicles onto operating leases and thus reduce the size of the bank overdraft.

Sale and leaseback

Similarly the company might be able to raise funds through a sale and leaseback of property which could be used to reduce the level of debt. There may also be some scope to reduce the level of working capital through improving inventory and receivable turnovers and increasing the amount of credit taken from suppliers. However, the opportunities are likely to be limited. For example, the average debt collection period could probably not be reduced much below the current level of 52 days.

Increasing shareholders' funds

A rights issue could be used to increase the size of shareholders' funds include the following. The reaction of the market to a rights issue will depend on the rating of the company and the purpose for which the issue is being made.

Reduction in interest charges

Since the loan was taken out at a time when interest rates were very high, to reduce the level of its interest charges the company could take one of the following options:

Redeem the loan notes and replace with additional overdraft

This would reduce the interest cost by £5m × (15% − 9%) = £0.3m

The interest coverage would then become:

£3m ÷ (£1.0m − £0.3m) = 4.3 times

However the bank may be unlikely to agree to such a large increase in the overdraft facility given the purpose for which the finance is required.

Redeem the loan notes and replace with medium-term bond

This would reduce the interest cost by £5m × (15% – 5%) = £0.5m

The improvement in interest coverage makes this option, which has been put forward by the finance director, appear attractive.

Task 7.15

(a) Hire purchase

A hire purchase agreement is an arrangement between a seller and a buyer of a capital asset, such as an item of equipment or a motor vehicle. The seller is often a finance house which purchases the asset from the manufacturer. The manufacturer delivers the asset to the HP buyer, and receives payment from the finance house.

The arrangement between the finance house and the buyer is for the buyer to make a series of regular hire purchase payments, which consist partly of payment of the purchase price for the asset and partly of interest charges. The buyer becomes the legal owner of the asset when the final hire purchase payment has been made. The buyer is responsible for maintenance of the asset and for normal repairs.

Hire purchase is a form of instalment purchase for a capital asset.

(b) Finance lease

A finance lease is similar in many respects to hire purchase, but there are also significant differences. A finance lease is an agreement between a lessor and a lessee for the 'renting' or leasing of a capital asset over a period of time that covers most of the expected useful life of the asset.

The lessor is often a finance house that purchases the asset from the manufacturer, and the manufacturer delivers the asset to the lessee. The lessor remains the legal owner of the asset throughout the period of the lease and can claim capital allowances. The lessee is not the owner, but pays regular lease rental payments. The lessee is also responsible for maintenance of the asset. A finance lease has a primary lease period, covering most of the expected useful life of the asset. At the end of this period, the lessor may take back possession of the asset and dispose of it in the market (sell it as a second-hand asset or dispose of it for scrap). Alternatively, the lessee may continue to lease the asset for a secondary lease period at a much lower rental cost, or may agree to buy the asset for the lessor.

(c) Operating lease

An operating lease has similarities with a finance lease. It is an agreement between a lessor and a lessee for the 'renting' or leasing of a capital asset, but the lease period is much less than the expected useful operational life of the asset. The lessor may be the manufacturer of the equipment, such as a manufacturer of photocopier machines or vending machines.

The lessor remains the legal owner of the asset. The lessor, not the lessee, is responsible for maintenance.

At the end of the operating lease period, the lessor takes back possession of the asset and may lease it to another business under an operating lease agreement, or may sell the asset. The lessee may enter into a new operating lease agreement, but for a more up-to-date item of equipment.

Task 7.16

Factors to be considered

In general, a bank wishes to ensure that the client will be able to make the scheduled repayments, in full and within the required period of time. A bank's decision whether to lend will be based on the following factors (choose any four).

(i) The purpose of the borrowing

The type of funds must be matched to the **purpose** for which they are required. For example, a **business expansion programme** is likely to **require finance** both for the purchase of additional non-current assets, and for an increase in the level of working capital. In general cheaper **short-term funds** should only be used to **finance short-term requirements**. Short-term debt, usually in the form of an overdraft, is repayable on demand, and it would therefore be risky to finance long-term capital investments in this way.

(ii) Ability to borrow and repay

Lenders need to be convinced of the client's ability to service the debt and to repay it at the end of the term. The client may need to provide financial statements, and put together a **business plan** that shows, for example, how earnings will be sufficient to cover interest costs, and also how repayment at the end of the loan period will be funded. The client must also confirm that it has the **legal capacity** to borrow in the manner required, by checking the company's constitution, and making sure that there is no breach of any restrictive covenants on existing borrowings.

(iii) **Repayment terms**

The **relative costs** of the alternative sources of finance must be considered. For example, short-term debt is usually cheaper than long-term debt, but will carry a higher level of risk. The **repayment terms** must also be **matched** to the pattern of expected cash flows. A bank should not lend money to a client which has not got the resources to repay it with interest. The timescale for repayment is also very important.

(iv) **Character of the borrower**

To assess this, the bank may look at the **client's past record** with the bank (if relevant), or conduct a personal interview. Key performance ratios may also be examined.

(v) **Margin of profit**

The bank needs to decide what **level of interest** to charge, in order to make money. The lending policies of most banks stipulate different rates for different purposes to customers. The interest rate charged will also depend on the **perceived risk** of the investment to the lender, and this is another reason for putting together a comprehensive business plan.

(vi) **Amount of the borrowing**

The bank must make sure of **exactly how much** the customer wishes to borrow, to be satisfied that it is lending neither too much nor too little for the purpose. This is especially important with requests for an overdraft facility. The bank's lending policy will indicate limits on the amount of certain loans, and the amount which must be paid up front by the client.

(vii) **Security**

As insurance, the bank might ask for the amount to be secured, by **fixed** or **floating changes** over assets. If the borrower defaults on repayments, the bank can attempt to obtain its money by selling the assets secured.

Task 7.17

Debt factoring is an arrangement to have debts collected by a factor company which advances a proportion of the money it is due to collect, usually up to 80% of the value of the debts. This is lent against the security of the client's trade receivables. The factoring company takes over the administration of the client's accounts receivable ledger, saving the client time and effort. The factor takes over the risk of loss from bad debts.

Invoice discounting is the purchase by the provider of the discounting service, of trade debts at a discount. The invoice discounter does not take over the administration of the client's accounts receivable ledger and the arrangement is purely for the advancement if cash. It is designed to alleviate a temporary cash shortage and tends to consist of 'one-off' deals.

As Fibre Clean Ltd is a small company and Mr Sykes is worried about how he will manage the administration of debt collection, factoring would probably be a better option. However he will also need to look at the costs involved in factoring in comparison to his present arrangements and depending on the savings made, if any, weigh these criteria against each other.

Chapter 8

Task 8.1

The three main factors that should influence any decisions regarding investment of surplus funds are:

- Risk
- Return
- Liquidity

When cash is invested there are two main risks. There is the risk that the value of the investment will fall and there is also the risk that the return from the investment will be lower than expected due to changes in market interest rates. When a business is investing surplus funds it will generally wish to invest in investments where the risk of loss is fairly minimal.

The return on an investment has two potential aspects, the income return and the capital return. Most investments will pay some form of interest or dividend which is the income return. However, most investments will also tend to fluctuate in value over time and this is the capital return (or capital loss). In general, the higher the risk of an investment the higher will be the expected rate of return and *vice versa*.

Liquidity is the term used for the ease and speed with which an investment can be converted into cash. Any investments which are widely traded on a market, such as the money markets, will be very liquid but investments such as a bank deposit account which requires three months' notice to withdraw the funds would not be a liquid investment. The more liquid an investment is the lower the return is likely to be as less liquid investments will pay higher returns to attract investors.

Task 8.2

	Will accept ✓	Working
Investment paying interest of £300 every 6 months.		Total return = £600 (2 × £300) Rate of return = 600/20,000 = 3%
Investment with a lump sum return of £800 at the end of one year	✓	Rate of return = 800/20,000 = 4%
Investment paying annual interest of £600 plus a bonus of 1% of the capital invested if the deposit is retained for 1 year	✓	Total return = £600 + £200 bonus (1% × 20,000) = £800 Rate of return = 800/20,000 = 4%

The business is likely to be able to earn a higher rate of return if the period of time that the capital is available to invest increases.

	✓
True	✓
False	

If the business wants to be able to withdraw funds on demand this is likely to increase the rate of return available.

	✓
True	
False	✓

Task 8.3

The correct answer is:

	✓
(i), (ii), (iii)	
(ii), (iii), (v)	
(iii), (iv), (v)	✓
(ii), (iv), (v)	

Task 8.4

	✓
Their price will rise.	✓
Their price will fall.	

Task 8.5

	Bank deposit	Gilt-edged securities
Increase in value		
Decrease in value		✓
No effect	✓	

Task 8.6

Security procedures for the safe custody of cash include the following:

Physical procedures – Any cash or cheques received must be kept safe at all times and must only be accessible to authorised individuals within the organisation. Therefore, cash should be kept under lock and key either in a cash box, lockable till or safe. Only authorised individuals should have access to the keys.

Checks for valid payment – Payments received in cash will, of course, be valid provided that any notes are not forged. However if cheques are accepted as payment then they must be supported by a valid cheque guarantee card and be correctly drawn up, dated and signed. If debit or credit cards are accepted then basic checks should be made on the card and signature and authorisation must be sought for payments which exceed the floor limit.

Reconciliation of cash received – When payments are received in the form of cash, cheques or debit and credit cards then a list of all cash, cheque and card receipts taken during the day must be kept. This list must then be reconciled at the end of each day to the amount of cash in the till, cash box or safe. The list may be manual as each sale is made or may be automatically recorded on the till roll as each sale is rung in.

This reconciliation should not be carried out by the person responsible for making the sales but by some other responsible official. Any discrepancies between the amount of cash recorded as taken during the day and the amount physically left at the end of the day must be investigated.

Banking procedures – Any cash, cheques and card vouchers should be banked as soon as possible and intact each day. This not only ensures the physical safety of the cash but also that it cannot be used by employees for unauthorised purposes. It also means that once the money is in the bank it is earning the business the maximum amount of interest. All cash should be banked as soon as possible but if it is not possible to bank it until the following day then either the cash must be left in a locked safe overnight or in the bank's overnight safe.

Recording procedures – For security purposes the paying-in slip for the bank should be made out by someone other than the person paying the money into the bank. The total on the paying-in slip should be reconciled to the till records or cash list for the day.

Task 8.7

Possible action	Strategy
Invest in marketable securities	(b)
Spend surplus cash	(c)
Repay surplus cash to owners	(a)
Retain cash for ease of availability	(d)

Justifications for answers

(a)   No further growth/no plans for further capital expansion.

Action: An increased or **special dividend** should be paid to shareholders; the company could also consider a **share buyback**, by means of which shares would be repurchased from the shareholders and cancelled.

Reason: If no further investments are planned, cash surplus to the needs of the business should be **returned to shareholders** so that they can use it for other investment opportunities. A small cash surplus should however be maintained.

(b)   Acquisition of manufacturer

Action: Invest the cash surplus in **marketable securities** (eg Certificates of Deposit, commercial paper) or bank deposits.

Reason: Such investments ensure that the company will make a **return on its money** while retaining sufficient liquidity for when it makes an acquisition.

(c)   Development of new product lines

Action: **Spend** the **cash surplus** on the proposed capital investments.

Reason: Unless there is some other possible use for the funds, eg to fund an acquisition, it will be better to use the cash surplus rather than borrowing to **fund the capital investment**, since the cost of debt finance is likely to exceed the return achievable on cash investments.

(d) Acquisition of manufacturer and development of product lines

Action: **Retain the cash** until required for the acquisition. Fund the new product lines by borrowing or raising additional equity finance.

Reason: The cash will be **needed at short notice** for the acquisition. It should be easy to raise finance for the new product lines from external sources.

....

Task 8.8

(a)

	Investment of £50,000	Interest 2% above base rate	Convertible within 60 days	Low/ medium risk	No shares
Option 1	✓		✓	✓	✓
Option 2	✓	✓		✓	✓
Option 3		✓	✓	✓	✓

(b)

Option 1	
Option 2	
Option 3	
None of the options	✓

(c) Attitudes to risk are generally categorised into three approaches.

Risk seeker

A risk seeker is a decision maker who is interested in the **best outcomes** no matter how **small** the **chance** that they may occur. They will choose the option which has the potential for the highest return, even if the risk is higher.

Risk averse

A risk averse decision maker acts on the assumption that the **worst outcome might occur**. If different investments offer the same return, they will choose the option with the least amount of risk involved. An alternative investment with higher risk would only be considered if it had a sufficiently higher expected return to compensate.

BPP LEARNING MEDIA

Risk neutral

A risk neutral decision maker prefers the most likely outcome. The decision can be made using probabilities to determine the expected value of the outcome – that is, based on what is **likely as a long-term average** and so no account is taken of whether the decision maker is risk averse or a risk seeker.

Given that the requirements of the company are that the investment is low or medium risk, the company can be said to be risk averse. The requirement to only invest in products that can be converted to cash within 60 days is another indication of an unwillingness to take risks.

Task 8.9

(a) Gilt-edged securities or gilts are   marketable   British Government securities.

They pay a   fixed   amount of interest and are available with varying maturity dates which is the date   on which they will be redeemed .

(b) The correct answer is

Gilt-edged stocks	**Bank deposit account**
No change	Increase

Both a bank deposit account and gilts carry a stated rate of interest. However, they will be affected differently by changes in base interest rates.

With the bank deposit account if base rates change then the interest payable on the deposit will also normally change. However, the interest rate on the gilts will remain the same.

(c) The correct answer is

Gilt-edged stocks	**Bank deposit account**
Decrease	No change

If interest rates increase the amount deposited in the bank account will not be affected and when the deposit matures the initial deposit will be the amount returned plus any accumulated interest.

However, gilts are marketable securities and as such their market value will fluctuate with changes in base rates. If the base rate of interest increases then the market value of any amount invested in gilts will fall. Whereas if market interest rates decrease the value of gilts will increase.

Task 8.10

	✓
£0.20	
£0.50	
£5.00	✓
£11.52	

Dividend yield = Dividend per share / Current share price.

Therefore Current share price = Dividend per share / Dividend yield

Therefore Current share price = £0.24 / 0.048 = £5.00

Task 8.11

The interest rate on the bank deposit account is 1.1% per quarter. This is equivalent to $(1.011_4 - 1) \times 100 = 4.47\%$ per annum.

The interest rate on the bond is 2.5% every six months. This is equivalent to 2.5% × 2 = 5% per annum

Deposit account

Advantages

- The deposit account is more flexible than the bonds which have a fixed date.

- If market interest rates increase the return on the deposit account may also increase.

Disadvantages

- The return offered is variable which means that if base rates fall, it may change.

- In light of the global financial crisis and the failure of some banks, the deposit account would be considered riskier than government bonds.

Government Bond

Advantages

The main advantage is that a government bond is usually considered to be risk free. The interest rate per annum is also higher than the deposit account interest. This rate will be fixed.

Disadvantages

Bonds are not as flexible because they cannot be cashed in early. It is also possible that market interest rates will rise meaning that the return on the bond could be below market rate.

Task 8.12

Although an organisation may operate a finance function covering all its financial activities, there is a distinction between financial control activities and treasury activities.

Financial control activities involve the allocation and effective use of resources. This includes:

(i)   Analysing performance (management accounting)
(ii)   Reporting results (financial accounting)
(iii)   Advising on investment appraisal

Treasury activities involve managing liquidity, obtaining suitable types of finance and investing surplus funds. This includes:

(i)   Advising on sources of finance/potential investments
(ii)   Financial risk management
(iii)   Liaising with financial stakeholders (banks/financial intermediaries)

Large companies use the financial and currency markets heavily. These markets are volatile and changes can have a significant impact on a company's financial position. The advantage of having a separate treasury department, even if the team is small, is that they will be specialists in treasury management.

Treasury department activities

If the finance department identifies a financial issue such as a cash flow deficit the treasury function can advise on appropriate methods of raising finance and liaise with the sources of this finance to get the best deal for the company.

Whereas financial control functions may exist at a variety of local levels in a large organisation, the treasury department will be centralised at the head office and this brings economies of scale and specialism (eg they are able to negotiate better terms by pooling cash for investment or by amalgamating the funding requirements of individual business units).

The treasury department will also have the specialised skills required to assess performance in cash management with reference to the risk, return and liquidity needs of the organisation.

Task 8.13

To: Director of SelfBuild Ltd
From: Assistant Accountant
Re: Investment of cash surplus

In the case of this cash surplus the issues are as follows:

1   This cash is needed to **pay for the factory**. Therefore the risk of loss must be minimised, even at the cost of lower returns during the period of investment.

2   The cash will be needed in **3 to 4 months**. Therefore it cannot be tied up for a longer period.

I have looked at the three possible investment opportunities and found the following in relation to risk and return:

(i)   **Treasury bills.** These are virtually risk free

        Purchased now and held for 91 days, they will give us a return of 1% (1000 –990/990) over the three months.

        This equates to a simple annual yield of 4% (1% over 3 months × 4).

(ii)   **Equities** are higher yield (10%) but with a far higher level of risk. We have no way of knowing how the share index will perform over three months and we may end up selling at a loss in order to release the cash. If the shares are sold before the dividend is declared we will lose the dividend.

(iii)   **A bank deposit account** will pay 3.5% per annum. This is slightly less than Treasury bills but is also virtually risk-free and only requires 30 days notice. If notice is not given, a month's interest will be lost.

The best option would appear to be the Treasury bills for 91 days. If at the end of that time the cash is not needed for another month it could be put into a bank deposit account.

Task 8.14

(a) The two central roles of the bank of England are to:

- Contribute to national monetary policy by setting the base rate of interest and undertaking quantitative easing measures

- Monitor the UK economy and take action, if necessary, to maintain its stability

(b) The Financial Policy Committee monitors risks to the stability and growth of the UK economy and recommends action to reduce or manage those risks where possible.

(c) The Prudential Regulation Authority monitors the finance sector of the economy (including banks, building societies, insurers, credit unions and major investment firms) with a view to promoting the safety and soundness of the firms in that sector. This in turn helps protect the general public, who for example may have savings or investments in those institutions.

Task 8.15

Investing surplus funds in a way that is profitable, liquid and safe in principle is an appropriate approach. However, investing the funds in an unethical business could have several negative implications for Hillside, including:

- Damage to its reputation with customers. It may lose future revenues if customers begin to mistrust Hillside because of their association with unethical business practices elsewhere.

- Damage to employee relations. Hillside's employees may not like their employer supporting worker exploitation elsewhere, and may become demotivated or even seek to leave. It may also dissuade potential new applicants from applying for vacant positions.

- It may concern the providers of finance. This could be because they are ethical investors who disapprove, or they may fear a reduction in the performance of Hillside as it loses customers.

- It may discourage suppliers from wanting to be associated with Hillside and disrupt the supply chain, or at least limit the choice of suppliers available.

AAT AQ2016 SAMPLE ASSESSMENT 1 CASH AND TREASURY MANAGEMENT

Time allowed: 2 hours and 30 minutes

Cash and Treasury Management (CTRM)
AAT sample assessment 1

Task 1 (8 marks)

Browne Ltd prepare their accounts to 31 March each year.

You have the following further information:

1. The operating profit for the year ending 31 March 20X8 was £499,000 and the profit after tax was £401,000.

2. The operating profit included depreciation of £124,000.

3. The trade receivables as at 31 March 20X7 was £118,888 and as at 31 March 20X8 was £99,400.

4. The trade payables as at 31 March 20X8 was £73,211 and as at 31 March 20X7 was £96,424.

5. There was an operating loss for the year ending 31 March 20X7 of £9,000

    Browne Ltd have been making losses for several years.

    The corporation tax rate is 20% and is payable 9 months and 1 day after year end.

    No corporation tax payments on account have been made.

6. The company purchased a non-current asset in the year ending 31 March 20X8.

    The carrying value of this non-current asset was £72,000.

    The depreciation rate is 25% and a full year's depreciation charge is made in the year of acquisition.

7. The company had an overdraft at 31 March 20X7 of £56,000.

Use the table below to determine the closing cash position as at 31 March 20X8 from the information provided. Use minus signs where appropriate. If an answer is zero, enter 0.

	£
Operating profit	
Change in trade receivables	
Change in trade payables	
Adjustment for non-cash items	
Purchase of non-current assets	
Tax paid	
Change in net position	
Opening cash	
Closing cash	

Task 2 (8 marks)

Cronin Ltd is launching two new products, Product A and B, in the next month.

Product A costs £49.00 to manufacture.

The company is setting the sales price with a mark-up of 20% on cost price.

(a)   What is the sales price of Product A?

£ [   ]

Product B also costs £49.00 to manufacture.
The company is setting the sales price with a 20% margin on cost price.

(b)   What is the sales price of Product B?

£ [   ]

The sales volume of Product A in Period 2 is forecast to be 85,000 units, using the regression line y = 75000 + 5000x (where x is the period).

(c)   What is the forecast sales volume of Product A in Period 12?

[   ] units

The company wants the sales revenue for Product B in Period 12 to match that predicted for Product A.

(d)   What sales volume of Product B would they need to sell in order to achieve this?

> | | units

···

Task 3 (10 marks)

Dre plc has provided the following partially completed cash budget for month 1 and month 2.

Further information has been provided to determine the cash inflows and outflows from the company.

- The company let out part of its premises with effect from month 2.

  The rental charge is £51,600 per annum and is payable in equal monthly instalments on the first day of the month.

- The company has got £2,000,000 invested in a fixed rate account, paying interest of 3% per annum.

  The company has elected to have this interest paid monthly.

- The company received payment for the sale of the non-current asset in month 1 and made a profit of £14,000.

  The asset originally cost £96,000 and has been depreciated by 50%. Ignore any VAT implications.

- To replace the above asset, the company purchased a replacement in month 2 for £108,000 and paid 55% in month 2. The remaining balance would be paid in eight equal instalments commencing in month 3. Ignore any VAT implications.

- In the last few months, the company has taken out a mortgage on their premises.

  The premises cost £6,000,000 and the mortgage was 80% loan to value. The mortgage is for a 20 year period and interest is charged on the initial balance at 3.5% per annum. Payments are made on a monthly basis.

- Dre plc prepared its VAT return for the previous quarter ending month 12.

  The sales for the quarter were £8,510,122 net with purchases of £4,340,122. The VAT rate is 20%. Any VAT payment or refund will be made or received in month 1.

- The bank balance in period 12 was £416,000.

Using the information provided, complete the cash budget for the company for Month 1 and Month 2.

Notes

- Cash inflows should be entered as positive figures.
- Cash outflows should be entered as negative figures (use brackets or minus signs).
- Round to the nearest whole pound throughout.
- If a cell does not require an entry, leave it blank.

Cash Budget	Month 1 £	Month 2 £
Receipts		
Sales receipts	8,672,444	8,843,672
Rental income		
Investment income		
Sale of non-current asset		
Total receipts		
Payments		
Purchases	(4,432,152)	(4,563,222)
Wages and salaries	(1,946,717)	(1,921,136)
General expenses	(867,000)	(870,000)
Mortgage payment		
VAT payment to HMRC		
Purchase of non-current assets		
Dividends payment		
Overdraft interest		
Total payments		
Net cash flow		
Opening bank balance		
Closing bank balance		

Task 4 (10 marks)

Conrad Ltd purchases its raw materials from a major supplier, McCaw Ltd, for £10 per unit.

Purchases (in units) were 38,000 for period 2 and 41,000 for period 3.
The forecast purchases (in units) for the next periods are as follows:

	Period 4	Period 5	Period 6	Period 7
Forecast purchases of raw materials (in units)	40,000	42,000	41,000	44,000

Conrad Ltd currently pays McCaw Ltd for its purchases as follows:

- Period of purchase: 20%
- Period following period of purchase: 40%
- Balance to be paid two periods following the period of purchase

A competitor to McCaw Ltd has started offering the same raw materials at a price of £9.30 per unit.

However, their payment terms are as follows:

- Period of purchase: 80%
- Period following the period of purchase: 20%

McCaw Ltd has realised that their competitor is undercutting their prices, and is now offering Conrad Ltd the following discounts and payment terms for period 4 and onwards:

Option 1: 10% discount for making a full payment in the period of purchase.

Option 2: 5% discount for making a payment of 50% in the period of purchase and the remaining 50% in the period following the period of purchase.

(a) **Calculate the forecast cash payments in periods 5, 6 and 7 under the current purchase and payments terms, and for each of the two new discount options now offered by McCaw Ltd.**

	Period 5 £	Period 6 £	Period 7 £
Current terms			
Option 1: 10% discount			
Option 2: 5% discount			

(b) **Under the current purchase and payment terms, what are the trade payables at the end of period 3?**

£ [ ]

Task 5 (12 marks)

The table below relates to EWTA, a government department involved in promoting safety on roads. The figures have been provided by the finance team on the actual receipts and payments from the last monthly reporting period against budget.

The following information has been provided by a colleague:

- The driving theory test fee has been reduced from £33 per test to £30 per test and this has not been taken into account in the budgeted figures.

- There has been a new system implemented for vehicle testing sales. Due to some initial set-up problems, the system has been unstable and unavailable for a number of days in the period.

- There has been a recent reduction in the bank base rate from 1.75% to 1.25%.

- To implement the new system for vehicle testing sales, the department has employed a large number of temporary workers.

- The new system for vehicle testing sales is heavily reliant on IT (information technology) and the project has taken longer than planned, resulting in additional charges.

- It is company policy to ignore variances that are within 12% of budget.

	Budgeted £	Actual £
Receipts:		
Cash sales from driving theory tests	4,500,000	3,825,000
Cash receipts from vehicle testing sales	5,125,000	3,850,000
Investment income	68,000	48,500
Total receipts	9,693,000	7,723,500
Payments:		
Wages and salaries	(1,150,000)	(1,413,000)
IT costs	(4,800,000)	(6,100,000)
Capital expenditure	(160,000)	(165,000)
Bank charges	(21,000)	(17,000)
Utility costs	(51,000)	(54,000)
Total payments	(6,182,000)	(7,749,000)
Net cash flow	3,511,000	(25,500)

Prepare a report for the Board of Directors which explains why the adverse variances in excess of 12% of the budget could have occurred. Your report should also include:

- **The percentage change in the variances**

- **Possible actions that could be taken to rectify these variances and to reduce the likelihood of recurrence**

Task 6 (32 marks)

(a) **For which one of the following is the Bank of England responsible?**

	✓
Setting short term interest rates	
Setting the Annual Percentage Rate for banks	
Setting the rate of corporation tax	
Setting the rate of VAT	

(b) **Which one of the following is the main function of liquidity management?**

	✓
Ensuring a business invests in capital expenditure	
Ensuring a business can meet its liabilities	
Ensuring a business has cash in the bank	
Ensuring a business makes a profit	

The following figures have been extracted from the financial statements of a company for the year ended 31 December 20X9.

Statement of profit or loss (Extract)	31 December 20X9 £
Sales	6,225,000
Cost of sales	3,875,500
Gross profit	2,349,500
Included in cost of sales is cash purchases	3,176,000

Statement of financial position (Extract)	31 December 20X9 £
Non-current assets	3,250,000
Inventories	513,000
Trade receivables	2,233,000
Cash	624,123
Non-current liabilities	458,000
Trade payables	64,000
Taxes payable	87,000

(c) **Calculate the following, showing your answers to the nearest whole day.**

The inventory holding period is [＿＿＿] days.

The trade receivables collection period is [＿＿＿] days.

The trade payables period is [＿＿＿] days.

The cash operating cycle is [＿＿＿] days.

(d) **Which of the following is a sign of overcapitalisation?**

	✓
An increase in trade receivables	
Increasing use of bank overdraft	
Falling profit margins	
Having high levels of cash	

(e) **Which of the following best describes over trading?**

	✓
Paying suppliers before payments are due	
Having large inventory levels	
Having an insufficient capital expenditure programme	
Having insufficient working capital and cash to support increased levels of trading	

(f) **What is the main role of a treasury function?**

	✓
Ensuring a business has the liquid funds it needs and invests surplus money effectively	
Preparing the Annual Report and Accounts for the business	
Calculating the tax payable by a business	
Setting the budgets for a business	

(g) **When inflation increases and interest rates rise, a borrower would prefer?**

	✓
A fixed Interest rate on a loan	
Available interest rate on a loan	
Has no preference	

(h) **If an investment has a high rate of return, what is the likely risk associated with it?**

	✓
Low risk	
Medium risk	
High risk	

(i) **Identify whether the following statement is true or false.**

Statement	True ✓	False ✓
A fixed charge is security on a loan supplied by a group of assets.		

(j) **Identify the liquid asset from the options below.**

	✓
Inventory	
Property	
Savings account	
Trade receivables	

(k) **Identify whether the following statement is true or false.**

Statement	True ✓	False ✓
The Bribery Act deals with all aspects of white collar crime.		

(l) **Which of the following types of business are covered by Money Laundering Regulations?**

	✓
Accountants only	
Solicitors only	
Both accountants and solicitors	

Task 7 (22 marks)

A company has a five year loan of £500,000 and an overdraft of £50,000. Shareholder funds amount to £1,500,000.

(a) **What is the gearing ratio?**

	✓
33.33%	
25.00%	
26.83%	
272.73%	

(b) **What is the annual flat rate of interest for a loan of £400,000 over ten years if the monthly repayments are £8,000?**

The annual flat rate of interest is ☐ %

(c) **What is the annual interest payable on £950,000 if the rate of interest paid is 3.75% above the base rate of 0.75%?**

The annual interest payable is £ ☐

A company has agreed a bank overdraft facility of £70,000 on the following terms:

- The current annual interest rate is 19%.

- The interest is calculated on the closing monthly overdraft balance and should be included in the next month's opening balance.

- Assume there are no differences in the monthly charges for the number of days in the month.

BPP LEARNING MEDIA

(d) **Calculate the monthly interest cost (to the nearest penny) for the next five months in the table below. Minus signs must be used to denote the bank overdraft and the interest to be charged.**

	Month 2 £	Month 3 £	Month 4 £	Month 5 £	Month 6 £
Forecast net cash flow	15,000	–15,000	30,000	–30,000	–20,000
Opening overdraft	–40,000				
Closing overdraft before interest					
Overdraft interest to be charged					

(e) **Identify whether the following statement is true or false.**

Statement	True ✓	False ✓
The Annual Percentage Rate is always lower than the nominal rate of Interest.		

(f) **Identify whether the following statement is true or false.**

Statement	True ✓	False ✓
Invoice Factoring passes control of the sales ledger and credit control function to the factoring company.		

A business has contacted a bank to arrange a loan and has been given three options for the interest rate: fixed, variable or semi-variable.

(g) **In times of increasing inflation, which would be the best option?**

	✓
Fixed rate	
Variable rate	
Semi-variable rate	

Task 8 (18 marks)

A company intends to raise capital of £3 million (£3m) to purchase a non-current asset.

After considering many possibilities, they have narrowed their options down to the following:

Option 1:

The company takes out a bank loan for £3m for three years with interest chargeable at 9% per annum on the initial loan and an arrangement fee of 1.75% of the initial loan. The agreed terms of the loan are that the interest is charged on a flat rate on the initial balance of £3m.

Option 2:

The company enters into a hire-purchase agreement for the non-current asset purchase of £3m.

The amount of interest payable on the £3m credit is £651,083.

There are 35 regular monthly repayments. There is also the option to purchase the asset in the last month for an additional fee of £197,318 and the company would choose to do this.

The term is 36 months with an APR of 12.9%.

Option 3:

Rather than purchase the non-current asset, the company chooses to lease it instead. The lease will be treated as an operating lease and the lease rental payments will be £1.5m per annum.

The finance director has asked you to prepare a report for each option, including the cost to the company together with its advantages and disadvantages. The report should also include the treatment of each option in the financial statements and how they affect the company's liquidity, gearing and credit rating.

Option 1: Bank Loan

Option 2: Hire-Purchase Agreement

Option 3: Operating Lease

Task 9 (22 marks)

A company has £1,200,000 invested in a one year fixed interest bond which pays 3.4% per annum. Due to working capital requirements, they need to withdraw the full amount at the end of the 11th month of investment. The penalty for early withdrawal is an additional loss of one month's interest.

(a) **What is the total amount of interest that the company will receive?**

£ _____

(b) **Identify whether each of the following statements is true or false.**

Statements	True ✓	False ✓
Investing in property is considered to be a low risk investment.		
When inflation rises, interest rates generally decrease.		
Treasury gilts are considered to be high risk investments.		
FSCS stands for Financial Services Compensation Scheme.		

A&B Ltd has purchased 7% Treasury Stock with a redemption date in 2018. The cost of the stock was £125 per £100 of stock.

(c)   What is the current interest yield?

	✓
5.60%	
7.00%	
12.50%	
8.75%	

A company has voted that it will distribute a dividend payout of £3,500,000. The share capital is £7,000,000 with a nominal value of £0.50 per share.

(d)   What is the dividend payable per share?

£ [   ]

A company has invested £5,000,000 in a five year fixed interest bond at 4.2% per annum. It had the option after the first year to withdraw the interest paid in the first year or to add it to the initial investment. The company voted not to withdraw the first year's interest.

(e)   Calculate the interest paid for the year at the end of year 2.

£ [   ]

(f)   Identify whether the following statement is true or false.

Statement	True ✓	False ✓
A risk-averse investor is likely to invest in high risk investments.		

A company is to pay a dividend of £2.50 per share and the current market price of each share is £28.80.

(g)   What is the dividend yield per share? Show your answer to TWO decimal places.

[   ] %

£2,500,000 is invested in a 90 day notice period deposit account with a fixed rate of interest of 2.45% per annum.

(h)   What is the amount of interest paid in the first year?

£ [   ]

Task 10 (18 marks)

Payne Ltd has £3,000,000 available to invest in the following options:

Option 1:

A new mining company has a diamond mine in Central Africa and is offering shares at a price of £10.00 per share.

The research on this has shown that there is a strong possibility that this mine has an abundance of diamonds and therefore the shares could potentially rise to a value in excess of £100.00 per share. However recent media articles have stated that the mine does not have a robust health and safety policy and it is also guilty of using child labour.

Option 2:

A local company is looking to expand its business in the local area and to finance this programme is looking for investors to purchase shares at a discounted rate of £15.00 per share. The expansion plan is to create 250 new jobs in the local community which has a high unemployment rate.

Option 3:

A five-year fixed rate bond with a High Street bank paying interest of 5% per annum.

Write a report to Payne Ltd's finance director discussing the potential risks and rewards of investing in each of the options. For example, you could consider any ethical or moral issue(s) that may need to be taken into account when deciding whether or not to invest, or any benefits there might be for the local economy, if relevant.

Report to the finance director

AAT AQ2016 SAMPLE ASSESSMENT 1
CASH AND TREASURY
MANAGEMENT

ANSWERS

Cash and Treasury Management (CTRM)
AAT sample assessment 1

Task 1 (8 marks)

	£
Operating profit	499,000
Change in trade receivables	19,488
Change in trade payables	–23,213
Adjustment for non-cash items	124,000
Purchase of non-current assets	–96,000
Tax paid	0
Change in net position	523,275
Opening cash	–56,000
Closing cash	467,275

Task 2 (8 marks)

Cronin Ltd is launching two new products, Product A and B, in the next month.

Product A costs £49.00 to manufacture.
The company is setting the sales price with a mark-up of 20% on cost price.

(a)   What is the sales price of Product A?

£ | 58.80

Product B also costs £49.00 to manufacture.
The company is setting the sales price with a 20% margin on cost price.

(b)   What is the sales price of Product B?

£ | 61.25

The sales volume of Product A in Period 2 is forecast to be 85,000 units, using the regression line y = 75000 + 5000x (where x is the period).

(c)   What is the forecast sales volume of Product A in Period 12?

135,000 | units

The company wants the sales revenue for Product B in Period 12 to match that predicted for Product A.

(d) **What sales volume of Product B would they need to sell in order to achieve this?**

| 129,600 | units

Task 3 (10 marks)

Cash Budget	Month 1 £	Month 2 £
Receipts:		
Sales receipts	8,672,444	8,843,672
Rental income		4,300
Investment income	5,000	5,000
Sale of non-current asset	62,000	
Total receipts	8,739,444	8,852,972
Payments:		
Purchases	(4,432,152)	(4,563,222)
Wages and salaries	(1,946,717)	(1,921,136)
General expenses	(867,000)	(870,000)
Mortgage payment	(34,000)	(34,000)
VAT payment to HMRC	(834,000)	
Purchase of non-current assets		(59,400)
Dividends payment		
Overdraft interest		
Total payments	(8,113,869)	(7,447,758)
Net cash flow	625,575	1,405,214
Opening bank balance	416,000	1,041,575
Closing bank balance	1,041,575	2,446,789

Task 4 (10 marks)

(a) **Calculate the forecast cash payments in periods 5, 6 and 7 under the current purchase and payments terms, and for each of the two new discount options now offered by McCaw Ltd.**

	Period 5 £	Period 6 £	Period 7 £
Current terms	408,000	410,000	420,000
Option 1: 10% discount	542,000	369,000	396,000
Option 2: 5% discount	553,500	394,250	403,750

(b) **Under the current purchase and payment terms, what are the trade payables at the end of period 3?**

£	480,000

Task 5 (12 marks)

The notes below cover a range of possible points that you may include in your written response. These examples are not intended to be exhaustive and other valid comments may be relevant.

Cash sales from driving theory tests

- The cash sales from driving theory tests have decreased by £675,000 and this equates to an adverse variance of 15.00%.

- The cash sales have decreased because there has been a price reduction from £33 to £30 and this has not been budgeted for.

- Downturn in sales volumes.

- Possible timing difference, the volume might improve in future months.

- Inaccurate forecasting

- The remedy would be to amend future budgets taking into account price reduction.

- Public awareness campaign

Cash receipts from vehicle testing sales

- The cash receipts from Slot Sales are £1,275,000 under budget and this equates to an adverse variance of 24.88%.

- The reason for this is due to the new system which has been unavailable for a number of days in the period and therefore sales could not be taken.

- No remedy may be needed as future months should fall back in line with budget if the system is available.

- Inaccurate forecasting

- Downturn in volumes

- The remedy would be to monitor for next two months if system is available, next month may see a spike in sales to catch up but the following month should be back to normal.

Investment income

- Receipts from investment income are £19,500 below budget and this equates to an adverse variance of 28.68%.

- This is due to a drop in the bank base rate from 1.75% to 1.25% which has affected the rate of interest of the investment.

- Inaccurate forecasting. The remedy would be to amend future budgets until the rate changes again.

- Research other investments for a better return

Wages and salaries

- Wages and Salaries are overspent by £263,000 and this equates to an adverse variance of 22.87%.

- This is due to the new slot sales system where we have used a large amount of contingent labour.

- There is also the possibility that overtime has been used to catch up on the backlog when the system was unavailable.

- Inaccurate forecasting

- The remedy would be to increase the budget if the contingent labour workforce is still in place.

IT Costs

- IT Costs are overspent by £1,300,000 and this equates to an adverse variance of 27.08%.

- This is due to the new slot sales system where the project has over-run resulting in additional IT charges.

- Inaccurate forecasting
- The remedy would be to increase the budget if these increased costs are set to continue.
- Obtain up to date information from the project manager as to the future costs.

Banking Charges

- Banking Charges are under budget by £4,000 and this equates to a favourable variance of 19.05%.
- This could be due to the downturn in slot sales and the fact that the transactional volumes costs have reduced as a result of this.
- Inaccurate forecasting
- The remedy would be to review the company's cash receipts from slot sales for the next two months and you would expect transactional volumes to come back in line with budget.

Task 6 (32 marks)

(a) **For which one of the following is the Bank of England responsible?**

	✓
Setting short term interest rates	✓
Setting the Annual Percentage Rate for banks	
Setting the rate of corporation tax	
Setting the rate of VAT	

(b) **Which one of the following is the main function of liquidity management?**

	✓
Ensuring a business invests in capital expenditure	
Ensuring a business can meet its liabilities	✓
Ensuring a business has cash in the bank	
Ensuring a business makes a profit	

(c) **Calculate the following, showing your answers to the nearest whole day.**

The inventory holding period is [48] days.

The trade receivables collection period is [131] days.

The trade payables period is [33] days.

The cash operating cycle is [146] days.

(d) **Which of the following is a sign of overcapitalisation?**

	✓
An increase in trade receivables	
Increasing use of bank overdraft	
Falling profit margins	
Having high levels of cash	✓

(e) **Which of the following best describes over trading?**

	✓
Paying suppliers before payments are due	
Having large inventory levels	
Having an insufficient capital expenditure programme	
Having insufficient working capital and cash to support increased levels of trading	✓

(f) **What is the main role of a treasury function?**

	✓
Ensuring a business has the liquid funds it needs and invests surplus money effectively	✓
Preparing the Annual Report and Accounts for the business	
Calculating the tax payable by a business	
Setting the budgets for a business	

(g) **When inflation increases and interest rates rise, a borrower would prefer?**

	✓
A fixed Interest rate on a loan	✓
Available interest rate on a loan	
Has no preference	

(h) **If an investment has a high rate of return, what is the likely risk associated with it?**

	✓
Low risk	
Medium risk	
High risk	✓

(i) **Identify whether the following statement is true or false.**

Statement	True ✓	False ✓
A fixed charge is security on a loan supplied by a group of assets.		✓

(j) **Identify the liquid asset from the options below.**

	✓
Inventory	
Property	
Savings account	✓
Trade receivables	

(k) **Identify whether the following statement is true or false.**

Statement	True ✓	False ✓
The Bribery Act deals with all aspects of white collar crime.		✓

(l) Which of the following types of business are covered by Money Laundering Regulations?

	✓
Accountants only	
Solicitors only	
Both accountants and solicitors	✓

Task 7 (22 marks)

A company has a five year loan of £500,000 and an overdraft of £50,000. Shareholder funds amount to £1,500,00.

(a) What is the gearing ratio?

	✓
33.33%	
25.00%	
26.83%	✓
272.73%	

(b) What is the annual flat rate of interest for a loan of £400,000 over ten years if the monthly repayments are £8,000?

The annual flat rate of interest is [14] %

(c) What is the annual interest payable on £950,000 if the rate of interest paid is 3.75% above the base rate of 0.75%?

The annual interest payable is £ [42,750]

A company has agreed a bank overdraft facility of £70,000 on the following terms:

- The current annual interest rate is 19%.

- The interest is calculated on the dosing monthly overdraft balance and should be included in the next month's opening balance.

- Assume there are no differences in the monthly charges for the number of days in the month.

BPP
LEARNING MEDIA

(d) **Calculate the monthly interest cost (to the nearest penny) for the next five months in the table below. Minus signs must be used to denote the bank overdraft and the interest to be charged.**

	Month 2 £	Month 3 £	Month 4 £	Month 5 £	Month 6 £
Forecast net cash flow	15,000	–15,000	30,000	-30,000	–20,000
Opening overdraft	–40,000	–25,395.83	–41,035.43	–11,210.06	–41,862.66
Closing overdraft before interest	–25,000	–40,395.83	–11,035.43	–41,210.16	–61,862.66
Overdraft interest to be charged	–395.83	–639.6	–174.73	–652.49	–979.49

(e) **Identify whether the following statement is true or false.**

Statement	True ✓	False ✓
The Annual Percentage Rate is always lower than the nominal rate of interest.		✓

(f) **Identify whether the following statement is true or false.**

Statement	True ✓	False ✓
Invoice Factoring passes control of the sales ledger and credit control function to the factoring company.	✓	

A business has contacted a bank to arrange a loan and has been given three options for the interest rate: fixed, variable or semi-variable.

(g) **In times of increasing inflation, which would be the best option?**

	✓
Fixed rate	✓
Variable rate	
Semi-variable rate	

Task 8 (18 marks)

> The notes below cover a range of possible points that you may include in your written response.
>
> These examples are not intended to be exhaustive and other valid comments may be relevant.

Option 1 – Bank Loan

This will increase non-current asset levels by £3m in the Statement of financial position.

Cost of Loan:
Set Up Cost £3,000,000 × 1.75% = £52,500
Annual Interest £3,000,000 × 9% = £270,000
Total Interest £270,000 × 3 = £810,000
Total Cost of Loan £862,500
Monthly repayment is £3,810,000/36 = £105,833
1st month is £105,833 + £52,500 = £158,333

Advantages of Loan:

Generally loans can be tailored to suit the business eg period, repayment schedule and interest rates.

Generally lower interest rates than other finance options.

The repayments are fixed so good for budgeting purposes.

Payment holidays may be allowed.

Disadvantages of Loan:

Interest charged on the initial loan balance so no account taken of payments made.
Penalties for early repayment.

Security may be needed.
Covenants may be needed.
Charge may be placed on asset or asset(s).

Accounting Treatment:

The set-up fee and interest for year 1 will be charged to the statement of profit or loss in year 1 and the interest for years 2 and 3 will be charged to the statement of profit or loss in years 2 and 3.

The credit rating may suffer.

The balance of the loan will be split between current and non-current liabilities in the statement of financial position.

Only the current liability amount will have a bearing on the liquidity ratio.

The total amount of the balance outstanding on the loan will be included in the gearing calculation.

The gearing of the company will increase which could affect the company's ability to raise additional finance.

Option 2 – Hire Purchase Agreement

This will increase non-current asset levels by £3m in the Statement of financial position.

Cost of HP Agreement:
Total Interest £651,083
35 monthly repayments of £98,679 = £3,453,765
Option to Purchase Fee £197,318
Total Cost of HP Agreement £3,651,083
35 monthly repayments of £98,679 approx.
This is the cheapest option.

Advantages of HP Agreement:

As the interest is an APR it is calculated on a reducing balance.

Therefore the interest paid is less than the bank loan.

The company gets possession of the goods without paying the full price for them at the outset.

The repayments are fixed so good for budgeting purposes.

Disadvantages of HP Agreement:

The company is only hiring the machine until the option to purchase fee is paid.

If the company misses one monthly payment then the non-current asset can be seized.

Generally an expensive way to purchase goods.

Finance company owns the non-current asset until the option to purchase fee is paid.

Accounting Treatment:

The non-current asset will be shown in the SOFP of the Company.

The interest for year 1 will be charged to the statement of profit or loss in year 1 and the interest for years 2 and 3 will be charged to the statement of profit or loss in years 2 and 3.

The amount of credit will be split between current and non-current liabilities in the SOFP.

Only the current liability amount will have a bearing on the liquidity ratio.

This could result in a lower credit score.

The total amount of the HP credit will be included in the gearing calculation.

The gearing of the company will increase which could affect the company's ability to raise additional finance.

Option 3 – Operating Lease

Cost of Operating Lease:
Annual lease rental payments £1,500,000
Monthly repayment is £1,500,000/12 = £125,000
Total Costs is £4,500,000 over the 3 years.
This is the most costly option.
The lease term is not given and therefore the total costs are unknown. However as the asset is an operating lease it implies there is a useful economic life of the asset post lease term.

Advantages of Operating Lease:
Off balance sheet
No effect to gearing or liquidity

Disadvantages of Operating Lease:
Possibility of paying for asset twice and therefore costs the business more.
No ownership of asset.
Commitment to make payments over lease term.
Risk and reward remains with lessor.

Accounting Treatment:

The lease rental of £1.5m per annum will be charged to the statement of profit or loss.

There will be no entries in the statement of financial position for the operating lease but has to be shown in a note detailing the non-cancellable annual commitments.

The operating lease is off balance sheet and the gearing will be unaffected.

Therefore the total debt on the balance sheet will be unaffected by the lease but a competent credit risk analyst will consider the size of the lease commitment and estimate a revised gearing position including the operating lease as finance.

There will be no entry in current liabilities and the liquidity will be unaffected.

Task 9 (22 marks)

A company has £1,200,000 invested in a one year fixed interest bond which pays 3.4% per annum. Due to working capital requirements, they need to withdraw the full amount at the end of the 11th month of investment The penalty for early withdrawal is an additional loss of one month's interest.

(a) **What is the total amount of interest that the company win receive?**

£	34,000

(b) **Identify whether each of the following statements is true or false.**

Statements	True ✓	False ✓
Investing in property is considered to be a low risk investment.		✓
When inflation rises, interest rates generally decrease.		✓
Treasury gilts are considered to be high risk investments.		✓
FSCS stands for Financial Services Compensation Scheme.	✓	

A&B Ltd has purchased 7% Treasury Stock with a redemption date in 2018. The cost of the stock was £125 per £100 of stock.

(c) **What is the current interest yield?**

	✓
5.60%	✓
7.00%	
12.50%	
8.75%	

A company has voted that it will distribute a dividend payout of £3,500.000. The share capital is £7,000,000 with a nominal value of £0.50 per share.

(d) **What is the dividend payable per share?**

£	0.25

A company has invested £5,000,000 in a five year fixed interest bond at 4.2% per annum. It had the option after the first year to withdraw the interest paid in the first year or to add it to the initial investment. The company voted not to withdraw the first years interest.

(e) **Calculate the interest paid for the year at the end of year 2.**

£	218,820

(f) **Identify whether the following statement is true or false.**

Statement	True ✓	False ✓
A risk-averse investor is likely to invest in high risk investments.		✓

A company is to pay a dividend of £2.50 per share and the current market price of each share is £28.80.

(g) **What is the dividend yield per share? Show your answer to TWO decimal places.**

8.68	%

£2,500,000 is invested in a 90 day notice period deposit account with a fixed rate of interest of 2.45% per annum.

(h) **What is the amount of interest paid in the first year?**

£	61,250

Task 10 (18 marks)

> The notes below cover a range of possible points that you may include in your written response.
>
> These examples are not intended to be exhaustive and other valid comments may be relevant.

Diamond Mine in Central Africa:

This is a very high risk investment
No definitive evidence to support how rich the mine is
Obtain a copy of the research article and review
However there is a potential of a large return if the mine is successful and shares rise
Is this a FTSE100 company?
If so shares can be easily traded
If not risk increases
Total investment could be totally lost
Review company history and previous results
Does the company usually distribute dividends?
Could be reputational damage if child labour being used
Could be reputational damage if poor H&S record and a disaster occurs
A visit to the mine would be appropriate given the size of the possible investment.
Investing in Central Africa is very risky with political uncertainty and high levels of corruption.
Not unknown for African governments to seize foreign assets
Uncertain inflation
What is the company attitude to risk

Local Company

This is also a high risk investment
Is this a FTSE100 company – probably not
If so shares can be easily traded
If not risk increases
Look at company profile and results
Total investment could be totally lost
Could be helping the local community re-generate
Creating 250 local jobs
If local economy rejuvenates then more disposable income for community to spend
What is the company attitude to risk
Discounted shares could rise in value
However if they do rise what will the chances of selling them be
Maybe stuck with them
Share value could drop
Company could become insolvent due to a number of factors

Will the consequence of the expansion increase the trade for Payne ltd, directly or indirectly

Five-year fixed rate bond with a High Street Bank

It is difficult to identify the risk on this investment as the interest rate is fixed and the return is guaranteed.

Historically banks were seen as safe investments.

However, that has changed and although governments have bailed out banks some may still fail.

Traditionally fixed rate accounts were seen as risk free from the perspective of the loss of capital value.

However in light of the global financial crisis there is a risk of loss of capital value if the deposit is not covered by a government backed guarantee scheme.

There is a risk that early redemption penalties may be imposed but this is usually a couple of month's interest and there is no risk to the capital.

The return is 5% per annum.

This return should be guaranteed assuming it is a large UK bank which will be supported by the UK government.

The liquidity will be dependent on the terms of the investment. The investment is for a fixed period, however it may be possible to redeem the investment early with a small interest penalty.

Therefore the investment is readily available.

May be possible to sell the bond before maturity.

AAT AQ2016 SAMPLE ASSESSMENT 2 CASH AND TREASURY MANAGEMENT

Time allowed: 2 hours and 30 minutes

You are advised to attempt sample assessment 2 online from the AAT website. This will ensure you are prepared for how the assessment will be presented on the AAT's system when you attempt the real assessment. Please access the assessment using the address below:

https://www.aat.org.uk/training/study-support/search

BPP PRACTICE ASSESSMENT 1
CASH AND TREASURY MANAGEMENT

Time allowed: 2 hours and 30 minutes

Cash and Treasury Management (CTRM)
BPP practice assessment 1

Task 1

(a) **Complete the table by ticking the correct boxes to show whether an item affects cash or profit.**

	Cash	Profit
Purchases on credit		
Purchase of non-current asset		
Prepayment of expenses		
Depreciation		
Payments to credit suppliers		
Payment into a business by its owner		

(b) There are many different types of cash flows.

Complete the table below by dragging and dropping the correct description to match the type of cash receipt or cash payment.

Transaction	Type of receipt or payment
Payments to suppliers	
Dividend	
Sale of non-current assets	
Receipts from cash customers	
Payment of wages	
Payment of insurance claim for damage caused by goods sold	

The drag and drop options are:

Capital
Exceptional
Irregular
Regular

(c) Extracts from a company's statement of profit or loss and statement of financial position are given below. These are prepared on an accruals basis and the business holds minimal inventory.

Summarised statement of profit or loss for three months to 31 March

	£	£
Sales revenue		200,340
Less purchases		(119,500)
Gross profit		80,840
Less expenses		
Wages	22,500	
Rent of office	18,000	
Office expenses	7,400	
Van expenses	6,800	
Van depreciation	3,200	
		(57,900)
		22,940

Extracts from the statements of financial position at 1 January and 31 March show the following:

Statement of financial position at	31 March £	1 January £
Trade receivables	20,100	25,600
Trade payables	4,800	2,100
Accruals – office expenses	500	350
Prepayments – van expenses	700	200
Prepayments – rent of office	3,000	2,000

Calculate the actual business cash receipts and cash payments for the quarter to 31 March.

	£
Sales receipts	
Purchases payments	
Wages paid	
Rent paid	
Office expenses	
Van expenses	
Van depreciation	

Task 2

(a) A company uses an industry wage rate index to forecast future monthly wage costs. The current monthly wage cost of £10,660 was calculated when the wage index was 110. The forecast wage index for June is 144.

If the company uses the forecast wage rate index, what will the wage cost for June be to the nearest £?

£15,350 ☐

£8,143 ☐

£13,955 ☐

£11,726 ☐

(b) A business has access to the following sources of information:

(i) Market data on average wage rises and inflation rates
(ii) Industry information on competitors' labour costs
(iii) Data on the labour costs of key suppliers
(iv) Production department's labour usage budget
(v) Current payroll information from HR department

Which are likely to be the most useful in forecasting the total cost of labour for the business?

(i), (iii) and (v) ☐

(i), (iv) and (v) ☐

(ii), (iv) and (v) ☐

All of the above ☐

(c) Complete the sentences below using the picklists.

Time series analysis is used in budgeting to estimate future figures based upon a past trend. A (1) [▼] can be used to determine the trend in a time series. The trend is the general (2) [▼] movement of the time series. In the additive model future figures can be budgeted by adjusting the trend for any (3) [▼]. The process of using historical information to estimate future figures is known as (4) [▼]. This assumes that the trend and any seasonal variations (5) [▼] in the future.

Picklist:

(1) cyclical average/moving average/multiplicative average

(2) short-term/long-term

(3) seasonal variation/random variation

(4) extrapolation/interpolation

(5) will apply/won't apply

....

Task 3

PL Ltd is a company which manufactures fence panels. Production is budgeted to be 7,100 units in July, 7,300 units in August and 7,600 units in September.

You are given the following information regarding the purchases for the company:

(1) The cost of a strip of wood is expected to remain at £0.20 per strip for the next six months.

(2) Each fence panel requires 25 strips of wood.

(3) Wood inventory at 30 June 20X6 are 160,000 strips valued at £32,000.

(4) The plan is to reduce inventory of wood to 150,000 strips at the end of August and 120,000 strips at the end of September.

(a) **Complete the table below to calculate the purchases budget in units and in £ for the three-month period ending in September.**

	Workings	July Strips of wood	August Strips of wood	September Strips of wood
Production requirements				
Opening inventory				
Closing inventory				
Purchases in units				
		£	£	£
Purchases in £				

All purchases of wood will continue to be paid for one month in arrears as at present. The payables amount at 30 June 20X6 for purchases of wood made during June was £33,500.

(b) **Complete the table below to calculate the payments made to suppliers in each of the three months ending in September.**

	July £	August £	September £

Each panel takes 20 minutes of labour time to manufacture and the production staff are currently paid £7.50 per hour. It is expected that this will increase to £7.80 per hour from 1 September 20X6.

(c) **Complete the table below to calculate the wages cost for each of the three months ending in September.**

	Workings	July £	August £	September £

. . . .

Task 4

The cash budget for GI Ltd for the three months ended September has been partially completed. The following information is to be incorporated and the cash budget completed.

Additional information

- Fixed production overheads are expected to remain at £14,000 for July 20X6 which includes £4,000 of depreciation. The overheads other than depreciation are expected to increase by 5% from 1 August 20X6.

- Repairs and maintenance costs should be budgeted at an average of £2,500 per month.

- Sales department costs are expected to be £4,000 per month including depreciation of £800 per month.

- Capital expenditure of £20,000 should be budgeted for in August 20X6.

- The cash balance at 30 June 20X6 was £23,900.

Using the additional information above, complete the cash budget for GI Ltd for the three months ending in September. Cash inflows should be entered as positive figures and cash outflows as negative figures. Zeroes must be entered where appropriate to achieve full marks.

Cash budget for three months ending 30 September 20X6

	July £	August £	September £
Receipts:			
Receipts from customers	**104,697**	**106,284**	**109,296**
Payments:			
Payments to suppliers	–50,200	–52,600	–51,400
Wages	–21,300	–21,900	–23,700
Production overheads			
Selling overheads			
Repairs and maintenance			
Capital expenditure			
Total payments			
Net cash flow			
Opening cash balance			
Closing cash balance			

Task 5

A cash budget has been prepared for KL Ltd for the next five periods.

The budget was prepared based on the following sales volumes and a selling price of £10 per item.

	Period 1	Period 2	Period 3	Period 4	Period 5
Sales volume (items)	1,400	1,500	1,450	1,390	1,300

The pattern of cash receipts used in the budget assumed 60% of sales were paid for by customers in the month following the sale and the remaining 40% of customers paid two months after the sale.

The company is considering introducing a settlement discount of 2% for payments made in the month of the sale. This policy is expected to result in 50% of customers paying in the month of the sale, 10% paying in the month following the sale and the remaining 40% paying two months following the sale.

BPP
LEARNING MEDIA

(a) **Complete the table below to calculate the forecast receipts from customers for each of periods 3, 4 and 5 under the current payment system from customers.**

	Workings	Period 3 £	Period 4 £	Period 5 £
Total receipts from customers				

(b) **Complete the table below to calculate the forecast receipts from customers for each of periods 3, 4 and 5 if the system of settlement discounts is introduced.**

	Workings	Period 3 £	Period 4 £	Period 5 £
Total receipts from customers				

(c) **Complete the table below to show the effects of introducing the discount system.**

	Period 3 £	Period 4 £	Period 5 £
Original receipts from customers			
Revised receipts from customers			
Increase/(decrease) in sales receipts			

Task 6

(a) Given below is the cash budget for the three months ended 30 June 20X6 for an organisation. You are also given the actual cash flows for the three-month period.

Cash budget for the three months ended 30 June 20X6

	April £	May £	June £
Receipts from customers	91,500	96,700	92,400
Payments to suppliers	−31,400	−28,800	−30,100
Wages	−16,250	−16,500	−16,750
Production overheads	−10,000	−10,000	−10,000
Selling overheads	−3,300	−3,000	−3,000
Repairs and maintenance	−1,100	−1,500	−1,100
Capital expenditure	0	0	0
Dividend	–	–	−30,000
Cash flow for the month	29,450	36,900	1,450
Opening cash balance	41,100	70,550	107,450
Closing cash balance	70,550	107,450	108,900

Actual cash flows

The actual cash flows for each of the three months ended 30 June 20X6 were as follows:

	April £	May £	June £
Receipts from customers	86,500	91,200	84,400
Payments to suppliers	−33,200	−33,200	−32,700
Wages	−16,250	−16,500	−16,750
Production overheads	−10,000	−10,000	−10,000
Selling overheads	−3,100	−3,400	−3,500
Repairs and maintenance	−4,100	−3,900	−2,700
Capital expenditure		−50,000	
Dividend	−	−	−30,000
Cash flow for the month	19,850	−25,800	11,250
Opening cash balance	41,100	60,950	35,150
Closing cash balance	60,950	35,150	23,900

Prepare a reconciliation of the budgeted cash balance with the actual cash balance at 30 June 20X6. Select the appropriate description for each entry by highlighting it. Clearly indicate whether figures are to be added or deducted in the reconciliation by entering minus signs where appropriate.

	£
Budgeted closing cash balance	
Surplus/shortfall in receipts from customers	
Increase/decrease in payments to suppliers	
Increase/decrease in selling overheads	
Increase/decrease in repairs and maintenance	
Increase/decrease in capital expenditure	
Actual closing cash balance	

(b) **For each of the following significant deviations from a cash budget suggest one possible course of action that could have been taken to avoid the variance.**

Deviation in receipts from customers

Deviation in payments to suppliers

Change in repairs and maintenance payments

Change in capital expenditure

Task 7

(a) XYZ Ltd currently has a cash operating cycle of 35 days. It plans to introduce a new product range which will increase the inventory holding period by 5 days and increase the time taken to collect cash from customers by 14 days.

What is the new cash operating cycle? ☐ **days.**

(b) **The cash operating cycle is the period of time that a business takes to pay its suppliers.**

	✓
True	
False	

(c) Complete the sentences below using the picklists.

A business that is overcapitalised has (1) [▾] working capital

for the scale of its operations. It is likely to have an (2) [▾] in

current assets and make (3) [▾] use of credit from suppliers.

Picklist:

(1) too much/too little
(2) over-investment/under-investment
(3) sufficient/insufficient

· ·

Task 8

A firm is planning to expand its production facilities. The expansion plans will require the purchase of new machinery at a cost of £50,000 and additional working capital of £20,000.

The following finance options are available:

Option 1

A bank loan of £50,000 secured on the new machinery, with a flat rate of interest of 7% p.a. The loan principal plus the total interest on the loan is to be repaid in four equal annual instalments.

The bank is also offering an overdraft facility of £20,000 which attracts an annual interest rate of 10%. The firm believe that they will require an overdraft for the first two years only, with an average balance of £10,000 in year 1 and £8,000 in year 2. Annual overdraft interest will be charged on the last day of the year.

Option 2

A bank loan of £75,000 secured with a floating charge on the firm's assets.

There is a capital repayment holiday for the first year and then capital is to be repaid in three equal instalments at the end of the second, third and fourth years.

An arrangement fee of £1,000 will be charged and is payable at the end of the first year.

The interest rate is fixed at 7.5% per annum. Interest is charged on the last day of the year, on the capital amount outstanding at the start of the year.

Under this option there will be no requirement for a bank overdraft facility.

Complete the tables below to compare the total finance cost of the two options and the timing of the payments.

	Loan interest £	Overdraft interest £	Arrangement fee £	Total cost £
Option 1				
Option 2				

	Year 1	Year 2	Year 3	Year 4
Option 1 Finance costs				
Option 1 Capital repayments				
Total Option 1				

	Year 1	Year 2	Year 3	Year 4
Option 2 Finance costs				
Option 2 Capital repayments				
Total Option 2				

Task 9

The Finance Director has asked you to prepare some tutorial notes for use in training a junior colleague. The notes are to explain the main features of factoring and also of invoice discounting.

Tutorial notes

....

Task 10

A company has a cash surplus of £75,000 available to invest for 18 months before the capital will be required to construct a new production line.

The cash is currently held in a bank deposit account.

The company has decided to consider the following two options for its investment:

Option 1:

Invest in a mixed portfolio of shares and treasury stock. The minimum period of investment is 6 months; interest rate is 6% p.a.

Option 2:

Invest in a deposit account with an interest rate is 5% p.a. There is a penalty of 1% of capital invested for withdrawal before 12 months and a bonus of 2% of capital invested if the deposit is held for more than twelve months. At the end of the first year the bonus will be added to the capital amount and interest will be payable on the increased amount.

(a) Prepare an email to the finance director of the company comparing the risk and return of the two options and recommending a course of action for the company.

The portfolio of shares in option 1 includes a sports clothing manufacturer who maintains its low cost base by investing in a location with little environmental legislation. As a consequence it pollutes heavily (but within the law) as this reduces manufacturing costs.

(b) **Prepare a brief email to the finance director explaining the possible implications of investing in the sports clothing manufacturer.**

BPP PRACTICE ASSESSMENT 1
CASH AND TREASURY MANAGEMENT

ANSWERS

Cash and Treasury Management (CTRM)
BPP practice assessment 1

Task 1

(a)

	Cash	Profit
Purchases on credit		✓
Purchase of non-current asset	✓	
Prepayment of expenses		✓
Depreciation		✓
Payments to credit suppliers	✓	
Payment into a business by its owner	✓	

(b)

Transaction	Type of receipt or payment
Payments to suppliers	Regular
Dividend	Capital
Sale of non-current assets	Capital
Receipts from cash customers	Regular
Payment of wages	Regular
Payment of insurance claim for damage caused by goods sold	Exceptional

(c)

	£
Sales receipts	205,840
Purchases payments	116,800
Wages paid	22,500
Rent paid	19,000
Office expenses	7,250
Van expenses	7,300
Van depreciation	0

Workings

Sales receipts	=	200,340 + 25,600 – 20,100	=	205,840
Purchases payments	=	119,500 + 2,100 – 4,800	=	116,800
Rent paid	=	18,000 – 2,000 + 3,000	=	19,000
Office expenses	=	7,400 + 350 – 500	=	7,250
Van expenses	=	6,800 – 200 + 700	=	7,300
Van depreciation	=	0 (this is not a cash expense)		

Task 2

(a) The correct answer is £13,955

£10,660 × 144/110   =   £13,955

(b) The correct answer is (i), (iv) and (v)

(c) Time series analysis is used in budgeting to estimate future figures based upon a past trend. A (1) │ moving average │ can be used to determine the trend in a time series. The trend is the general (2) │ long-term │ movement of the time series. In the additive model future figures can be budgeted by adjusting the trend for any (3) │ seasonal variation │. The process of using historical information to estimate future figures is known as (4) │ extrapolation │. This assumes that the trend and any seasonal variations (5) │ will apply │ in the future.

Task 3

(a) Purchases budget

	Workings	July Strips of wood	August Strips of wood	September Strips of wood
Production requirements	7,100 × 25	177,500		
	7,300 × 25		182,500	
	7,600 × 25			190,000
Opening inventory		−160,000	−160,000	−150,000
Closing inventory		160,000	150,000	120,000
Purchases in units		**177,500**	**172,500**	**160,000**
		£	£	£
Purchases in £ (units × £0.20)		**35,500**	**34,500**	**32,000**

(b) Payments to suppliers

	July £	August £	September £
Opening payable	33,500		
July purchases		35,500	
August purchases			34,500

(c) **Wages payments**

	Workings	July £	August £	September £
July	7,100/3 × £7.50	17,750		
August	7,300/3 × £7.50		18,250	
September	7,600/3 × £7.80			19,760

Task 4

Cash budget for three months ending 30 September 20X6

	July £	August £	September £
Receipts:			
Receipts from customers	**104,697**	**106,284**	**109,296**
Payments:			
Payments to suppliers	–50,200	–52,600	–51,400
Wages	–21,300	–21,900	–23,700
Production overheads	–10,000	–10,500	–10,500
Selling overheads	–3,200	–3,200	–3,200
Repairs and maintenance	–2,500	–2,500	–2,500
Capital expenditure	0	–20,000	0
Total payments	**–87,200**	**–110,700**	**–91,300**
Net cash flow	17,497	–4,416	17,996
Opening cash balance	23,900	41,397	36,981
Closing cash balance	41,397	36,981	54,977

Task 5

(a)

	Workings	Period 3 £	Period 4 £	Period 5 £
	Period 1 sales 1,400 × £10 × 40%	5,600		
	Period 2 sales 1,500 × £10 × 60%	9,000		
	Period 2 sales 1,500 × £10 × 40%		6,000	
	Period 3 sales 1,450 × £10 × 60%		8,700	
	Period 3 sales 1,450 × £10 × 40%			5,800
	Period 4 sales 1,390 × £10 × 60%			8,340
Total receipts from customers		**14,600**	**14,700**	**14,140**

(b)

	Workings	Period 3 £	Period 4 £	Period 5 £
	Period 1 sales 1,400 × £10 × 40%	5,600		
	Period 2 sales 1,500 × £10 × 10%	1,500		
	Period 3 sales 1,450 × £10 × 50% × 98%	7,105		
	Period 2 sales 1,500 × £10 × 40%		6,000	
	Period 3 sales 1,450 × £10 × 10%		1,450	
	Period 4 sales 1,390 × £10 × 50% × 98%		6,811	
	Period 3 sales 1,450 × £10 × 40%			5,800
	Period 4 sales 1,390 × £10 × 10%			1,390
	Period 5 sales 1,300 × £10 × 50% × 98%			6,370
Total receipts from customers		**14,205**	**14,261**	**13,560**

(c)

	Period 3 £	Period 4 £	Period 5 £
Original receipts from customers	14,600	14,700	14,140
Revised receipts from customers	14,205	14,261	13,560
Increase/(decrease) in sales receipts	–395	–439	–580

224

Task 6

(a)

	£
Budgeted closing cash balance	108,900
Shortfall in receipts from customers	–18,500
Increase in payments to suppliers	–8,800
Increase in selling overheads	–700
Increase in repairs and maintenance	–7,000
Increase in capital expenditure	–50,000
Actual closing cash balance	23,900

(b)

Deviation in receipts from customers	Improve credit control procedures
Deviation in payments to suppliers	Negotiate better price or credit terms for payment
Change in repairs and maintenance payments	Arrange a fixed price maintenance contract
Change in capital expenditure	Delay expenditure or find an alternative method of (such as leasing)

....

Task 7

(a) 54 days

(35 + 5 + 14 = 54)

(b) False

The cash operating cycle is the period of time between cash being paid for raw materials and cash being received from customers for goods sold.

(c) A business that is overcapitalised has (1) [Too much] working capital for the scale of its operations. It is likely to have an (2) [Over-investment] in current assets and make (3) [insufficient] use of credit from suppliers.

Task 8

	Loan interest £	Overdraft interest £	Arrangement fee £	Total cost £
Option 1	14,000	1,800	0	15,800
Option 2	16,875	0	1,000	17,875

	Year 1	Year 2	Year 3	Year 4
Option 1 Finance costs	4,500	4,300	3,500	3,500
Option 1 Capital repayments	12,500	12,500	12,500	12,500
Total Option 1	17,000	16,800	16,000	16,000

	Year 1	Year 2	Year 3	Year 4
Option 2 Finance costs	6,625	5,625	3,750	1,875
Option 2 Capital repayments	0	25,000	25,000	25,000
Total Option 2	6,625	30,625	28,750	26,875

Task 9

Tutorial notes

Factoring

A factoring organisation specialises in trade debts, and manages the debts owed to a client (a business customer) on the client's behalf.

Factoring is an arrangement to have debts collected by a factor company, which advances a proportion of the money it is due to collect.

The factor

(a)   Administers the client's invoicing, sales accounting and debt collection service.

(b)   Takes over the risk of loss from bad debts and so 'insures' the client against such losses. This is known as a non-recourse service. However, if a non-recourse service is provided, then the factor, not the firm, will decide what action to take against non-payers.

(c)   Makes payments to the client in advance of collecting the debts. This is sometimes referred to as 'factor finance' because the factor is providing cash to the client against outstanding debts.

The benefits of factoring for a business customer include the following:

(a)   The business can pay its suppliers promptly, and so be able to take advantage of any early payment discounts that are available.

(b)   Optimum inventory levels can be maintained, because the business will have enough cash to pay for the inventories it needs.

(c)   Growth can be financed through sales rather than by injecting fresh external capital.

(d)   The business gets finance linked to its volume of sales. In contrast, overdraft limits tend to be determined by historical statements of financial position.

(e)   The managers of the business do not have to spend their time on the problems of slow paying accounts receivable.

(f)   The business does not incur the costs of running its own sales ledger department, and can use the expertise of receivables management that the factor has.

An important disadvantage is that credit customers will be making payments direct to the factor, which may damage the firm's relations with customers. It may also indicate that the firm is in need of rapid cash, raising questions about its financial stability.

Invoice discounting

Invoice discounting is the purchase (by the provider of the discounting service) of trade debts at a discount. Invoice discounting enables the company from which the debts are purchased to raise working capital.

Invoice discounting is related to factoring and many factors will provide an invoice discounting service. It is the purchase of a selection of invoices, at a discount. The invoice discounter does not take over the administration of the client's sales ledger.

A client should only want to have some invoices discounted when they have a temporary cash shortage, and so invoice discounting tends to consist of one-off deals. Confidential invoice discounting is an arrangement whereby a debt is confidentially assigned to the factor, and the client's customer will only become aware of the arrangement if they do not pay their debt to the client.

If a company needs to generate cash, it can approach a factor or invoice discounter, who will offer to purchase selected invoices and advance up to 75% of their value. At the end of each month, the factor will pay over the balance of the purchase price, less charges, on the invoices that have been settled in the month.

Task 10

(a)

Email

To: fd@company.co.uk   **Date**: Today

From: aatstudent@company.co.uk   **Subject**: Investment options

The company has £75,000 to invest for a period of eighteen months. As the investment is required for the construction of the new production line, it is important that we do not expose the company to too much risk.

If the company selects Option 1, the total return on the investment will be **£6,750**.

If the company selects Option 2, the total return on the investment will be **£7,162.50**.

The risk is higher with Option 1 and the return is lower.

I recommend that **Option 2** be selected as this will have the **highest return** for the company and the **lowest risk**. The return on investment for the eighteen month period will be **9.55**% (as opposed to 9% with Option 1).

Workings

Option 1: £75,000 × 6% × 18/12 = £6,750

Option 2:

Interest year 1 = £75,000 × 5% = £3,750

Bonus = 2% × £75,000 = £1,500

Interest year 2 = 5% × £76,500 × 6/12 = £1,912.50

Total Option 2 = £3,750 + £1,500 + £1,912.50 = £7,162.50

Increase return of £7,162.50/£75,000 = 9.55%

(b)

Email			
To:	fd@company.co.uk	**Date**:	Today
From:	aatstudent@company.co.uk	**Subject**:	Ethical implications

Further to my previous email, it may be prudent to recognise the fact that one of the securities being considered for option 1 includes investing in a sports clothing manufacturer that has a heavily polluting manufacturing process. Although this is not illegal in its place of manufacture, we should still be concerned as the ethical implications could affect us in several ways, for example:

Our customers, should they find out, may disapprove and choose to take their custom elsewhere.

Our employees may be demotivated as a result of our supporting a heavily polluting business partner and productivity and morale may drop as a result.

Our suppliers may wish to disassociate themselves from us in case their reputations are tarnished.

Our finance providers may be concerned about the damage to our reputation and what impact this may have on our financial performance.

Therefore, before a final decision is made on which option to take, these nonfinancial considerations should also be considered.

Thanks and regards

aatstudent

BPP PRACTICE ASSESSMENT 2
CASH AND TREASURY MANAGEMENT

Time allowed: 2 hours and 30 minutes

Cash and Treasury Management (CTRM)
BPP practice assessment 2

Task 1

The accountant of a company has prepared a budgeted statement of profit or loss for the month of April 20X6 and a statement of financial position as at 30 April 20X6.

Extracts from the statement of profit or loss are as follows:

	£
Sales revenue	170,000
Purchases	72,000
Factory rent	31,000
Administrative expenses	14,000
Delivery lorry expenses	16,000
Delivery lorry depreciation	3,000

Extracts from the statement of financial position at 1 April and 30 April are as follows:

	30 April	1 April
Receivables	39,000	32,000
Payables	15,000	17,000
Prepaid factory rent	7,000	6,000
Accrued administrative expenses	2,000	1,000
Accrued delivery lorry expenses	4,000	2,000

Calculate the actual cash receipts and payments for the month of April.

	£
Receipts for sales	
Payments for purchases	
Factory rent paid	
Administrative expenses paid	
Delivery lorry expenses paid	
Depreciation	

Task 2

A company is trying to estimate its production volumes for one of its products for the first three months of 20X6. This to be done by calculating a trend using the actual monthly production volumes for 20X5 and a 3-point moving average.

(a) **Complete the table below to calculate the monthly production volume trend and identify any monthly variations.**

	Production volume Units	Trend Units	Monthly variation (volume less trend) Units
January	90,000		
February	98,000		
March	112,000		
April	96,000		
May	104,000		
June	118,000		
July	102,000		
August	110,000		
September	124,000		
October	108,000		
November	116,000		
December	130,000		

The monthly sales volume trend is [   ] units.

(b) **Using the trend and the monthly variations identified in part (a) complete the table below for forecast sales volume for January, February and March of the next financial year.**

	Forecast trend Units	Variation Units	Forecast sales volume Units
January			
February			
March			

Task 3

Happy Chefs Ltd, a catering company providing catering and meals for corporate and private clients, is preparing its cash budget for the first three months of 20X6.

January credit sales will be £104,000, February should be £140,000 and March £155,000. Cash inflows from sales invoices will be as follows:

- 40% in the month the invoice is issued
- 50% in the month after the invoice is issued
- 10% two months after the invoice is issued

Receivables at 31 December 20X5 were £160,000 and of these it is anticipated that £125,000 will be received in January and the remainder in February.

From 1 February the company is opening a factory sales outlet for sales to the public of pre-packaged foods. In the early months sales for cash are expected to total £800 a month.

Complete the table below to calculate the receipts from sales for the three months ending in March.

	Workings	January £	February £	March £
Cash sales				
Opening receivables				
January sales				
February sales				
March sales				
Total receipts from sales				

....

Task 4

Happy Chefs Ltd needs to complete a budget for cash payments for the first three months of 20X6. It estimates that on average it earns a gross margin of 40% on the sale of meals and catering. The total cost of each meal is made up of 30% ingredients and 70% labour and overheads. The suppliers of ingredients are always paid one month after the month of purchase. Because ingredients are perishable, inventory is kept to a minimum.

Labour and overheads are paid in the month incurred.

Trade payables at 1 January 20X6 are £17,600.

(a) **Complete the table below to calculate cost of sales for the three months from January to March:**

	Workings	January £	February £	March £
Total sales		104,000	140,800	155,800
Cost of sales				
Split:				
Ingredients				
Labour and overheads				

(b) **Complete the table below to calculate the cash payments made in each of the three months:**

	January £	February £	March £	Trade payables at 31 March £
Payment to suppliers				
Payment for labour and overheads				
Total cash payments				

Task 5

A company is preparing its cash budget for the first three months of 20X6. The following information is known regarding forecast cash payments. The receipts have already been calculated and are given in the cash budget below.

- Purchases were £70,000 in December and are expected to be £41,600 in January, £56,000 in February and £62,000 in March. These purchases are paid for in the month after purchase.

- Salaries are currently £43,000 but are due to rise by 5% from 1 March.

- Administration costs will be £27,000 in January but due to a rent increase will go up by £3,000 from 1 February onwards.

 BPP LEARNING MEDIA

- The company is investing in new equipment and there is to be a down payment of £20,000 on 1 February and a monthly payment thereafter of £6,000.
- The cash balance at 31 December 20X5 was an overdraft of £39,400 (ignore any interest on the overdraft.)

Prepare a monthly cash budget for the company for the three months to March.

	January £	February £	March £
Cash receipts:			
Receipts from sales	153,400	148,800	145,600
Deposit account interest	100	100	100
Total cash receipts	**153,500**	**148,900**	**145,700**
Cash payments:			
Payments to suppliers			
Salaries			
Administration overheads			
Capital expenditure			
Total payments			
Net cash flow			
Opening cash balance			
Closing cash balance			

Task 6

Given below are the budgeted and actual cash flows for a catering company for the month of December 20X5.

(a) **Complete the table below to calculate each variance between actual and budget and state whether it is favourable or adverse.**

	Actual £	Budget £	Variance £	Fav/Adv £
Sales receipts	154,000	175,000		
Food costs	−72,500	−64,000		
Salaries	−43,000	−43,000		
Administrative costs	−25,400	−27,600		
Capital expenditure	−64,000	−18,000		
Dividend	−20,000	0		
Deposit account interest	100	100		
Net cash flow	−70,800	22,500		
Opening cash balance	31,400	30,000		
Closing cash balance	−39,400	52,500		

(b) **Suggest a possible cause for the Sales receipts, Materials costs, Administrative costs, Capital expenditure and Dividend variances and suggest four actions which could have reduced the overdraft.**

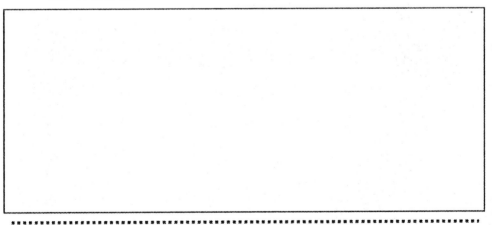

Task 7

(a) **Which of the following describes the cash operating cycle?**

Inventory – receivables + cash ☐

Receivables – payables + inventory + cash ☐

Cash + inventory – payables ☐

Receivables + inventory + cash + payables ☐

(b) **Selecting from the picklists complete the following sentences.**

Over-trading occurs when a business has [▾] working capital.

Over-capitalisation occurs when a business has [▾] working capital.

Picklist:

too little
too much

(c) **XYZ Ltd is able to exactly match its trade payables payment period with its trade receivables collection period. As a result its cash operating cycle depends purely on its inventory holding policy.**

	✓
True	
False	

(d) Extracts from the financial statements of QWE Co for the years ended 31 March are as follows.

	20X6 £000	20X7 £000
Inventories – raw materials	55	80
Inventories – finished goods	180	190
Purchases of raw materials	600	850
Cost of sales	1,570	1,830
Administrative expenses	45	65
Sales	1,684	1,996
Trade receivables	114	200
Trade payables	50	70
Overdraft	400	950
Additions to non-current assets	700	900

Cost of sales includes all relevant production costs including manufacturing overheads and labour.

Calculate the length in days of the company's operating cycle for the year ended 31 March 20X7. ☐

....

Task 8

(a) **What are the advantages of each type of financing In the table below?**

Type of finance	Advantages
Bank loan	
Overdraft	

(b) The directors of FH Panels Ltd have identified the opportunity to purchase a freehold property at a cost of £1,100,000. They will also require additional working capital for the project of £100,000.

What would normally be the best method of financing these two elements of the project? Tick the most appropriate row.

Freehold property	Working capital	✓
Overdraft	Overdraft	
Bank loan	Bank loan	
Bank loan	Overdraft	
Overdraft	Bank loan	

(c) Insert a tick in the table below to indicate the effect that certain actions by a company would have on any overdraft finance.

	Increase overdraft ✓	Decrease overdraft ✓
Increase inventory levels		
Improve credit control procedures		
Increase quantity of sales		
Drawings taken by the owner		

Task 9

Discuss the dangers to a company of a high level of gearing, including in your answer an explanation of the following terms:

(i)   Business risk

(ii)   Financial risk

Task 10

A company has an investment policy which specifies the following:

*   Investments must be medium-low risk.
*   The maximum to be invested in a single investment is £50,000.
*   The minimum required return is 3% p.a.
*   An investment must be convertible into cash within 1 month.

The company has £100,000 to invest and is considering the following options:

Option 1:

Minimum investment £60,000, interest rate 3.9% p.a., 30 day notice period, the majority of the investment is held in Treasury stock, with a small amount in shares of FTSE 100 quoted companies.

Option 2:

No minimum investment, interest rate 3% p.a., investment in Gilts.

Option 3:

Minimum investment £50,000; bank deposit account, interest rate 3.5% p.a., 30 day notice period.

Option 4:

No minimum investment, investment in portfolio of shares in quoted companies, interest rate 4.5% p.a., no notice period

(a) **Assess whether the investment options comply with the company's investment policy and recommend an appropriate investment strategy for the company, showing the investments in order of preference**

The company's investment policy also requires all its employees to fully comply with the UK Bribery Act 2010 in the execution of the policy.

(b)   What are the main provisions of the UK Bribery Act 2010?

BPP PRACTICE ASSESSMENT 2
CASH AND TREASURY MANAGEMENT

ANSWERS

Cash and Treasury Management (CTRM)
BPP practice assessment 2

Task 1

	£
Receipts for sales	163,000
Payments for purchases	74,000
Factory rent paid	32,000
Administrative expenses paid	13,000
Delivery lorry expenses paid	14,000
Depreciation	0

Workings

Receipts for sales	=	170,000 + 32,000 – 39,000	=	163,000
Payments for purchases	=	72,000 + 17,000 – 15,000	=	74,000
Factory rent paid	=	31,000 – 6,000 + 7,000	=	32,000
Administrative expenses	=	14,000 + 1,000 – 2,000	=	13,000
Lorry expenses	=	16,000 + 2,000 – 4,000	=	14,000
Depreciation	=	0 (this is not a cash expense)		

Task 2

(a)

	Production volume Units	Trend Units	Monthly variation (volume less trend) Units
January	90,000		
February	98,000	100,000	–2,000
March	112,000	102,000	+10,000
April	96,000	104,000	–8,000
May	104,000	106,000	–2,000
June	118,000	108,000	+10,000
July	102,000	110,000	–8,000
August	110,000	112,000	–2,000
September	124,000	114,000	+10,000
October	108,000	116,000	–8,000
November	116,000	118,000	–2,000
December	130,000		

The monthly sales volume trend is $\boxed{2,000}$ units.

(This is calculated as (£118,000 – £100,000)/9 interval gaps).

(b)

	Forecast trend Units	Variation Units	Forecast sales volume Units
January (118,000 + (2 × 2000))	122,000	–8,000	114,000
February (118,000 + (3 × 2,000)	124,000	–2,000	122,000
March (118,000 + (4 × 3,000))	126,000	+10,000	136,000

Task 3

	Workings	January £	February £	March £
Cash sales			800	800
Opening receivables		125,000	35,000	
January sales	104,000 × 40%	41,600		
	104,000 × 50%		52,000	
	104,000 × 10%			10,400
February sales	140,000 × 40%		56,000	
	140,000 × 50%			70,000
March sales	155,000 × 40%			62,000
Total receipts from sales		**166,600**	**143,800**	**143,200**

Task 4

(a)

	Workings	January £	February £	March £
Total sales		104,000	140,800	155,800
Cost of sales	104,000 × 0.6	62,400		
	140,800 × 0.6		84,480	
	155,800 × 0.6			93,480
Split:				
Ingredients	62,400 × 0.3	18,720		
	84,480 × 0.3		25,344	
	93,480 × 0.3			28,044
Labour and overheads	62,400 × 0.7	43,680		
	84,480 × 0.7		59,136	
	93,480 × 0.7			65,436

(b)

	January £	February £	March £	Trade payables at 31 March £
Payment to suppliers	17,600	18,720	25,344	28,044
Payment for labour and overheads	43,680	59,136	65,436	
Total cash payments	61,280	77,856	90,780	

Task 5

	January £	February £	March £
Cash receipts:			
Receipts from sales	153,400	148,800	145,600
Deposit account interest	100	100	100
Total cash receipts	**153,500**	**148,900**	**145,700**
Cash payments:			
Payments to suppliers	–70,000	–41,600	–56,000
Salaries	–43,000	–43,000	–45,150
Administration overheads	–27,000	–30,000	–30,000
Capital expenditure		–20,000	–6,000
Total payments	**–140,000**	**–134,600**	**–137,150**
Net cash flow	**13,500**	**14,300**	**8,550**
Opening cash balance	–39,400	–25,900	–11,600
Closing cash balance	**–25,900**	**–11,600**	**–3,050**

Task 6

(a)

	Actual £	Budget £	Variance £	Fav/Adv £
Sales receipts	154,000	175,000	21,000	Adv
Food costs	–72,500	–64,000	8,500	Adv
Salaries	–43,000	–43,000	0	
Administrative costs	–25,400	–27,600	2,200	Fav
Capital expenditure	–64,000	–18,000	46,000	Adv
Dividend	–20,000	0	20,000	Adv
Deposit account interest	100	100	0	
Net cash flow	–70,800	22,500	93,300	Adv
Opening cash balance	31,400	30,000	1,400	Fav
Closing cash balance	–39,400	52,500	91,900	Adv

(b) Cause

- Sales receipts – Loss of customers
- Materials costs – Increase in suppliers prices
- Administrative costs – Cost cutting
- Capital expenditure – Unplanned expenditure
- Dividend – Unplanned discretionary payment

Actions to reduce overdraft:

- Delayed payments to suppliers
- Delayed capital expenditure
- Delayed dividend
- Took out a bank loan for capital expenditure

Task 7

(a) Receivables – payables + inventory + cash

(b) Over-trading occurs when a business has ┌ too little ┐ working capital.

Over-capitalisation occurs when a business has ┌ too much ┐ working capital.

(c) True

(d) **Length of operating cycle** = 365 × (average raw materials/Purchases + Average finished goods/Cost of sales + Average receivables/Sales + Average payables/Purchases)

$0.5(55 + 80)/850 \times 365 = 29.0$ days
$0.5(180 + 190)/1,830 \times 365 = 36.9$ days
$0.5(114 + 200)/1,996 \times 365 = 28.7$ days
$0.5(50 +70)/850 \times 365 = 25.8$ days
Operating cycle = 29.0 days + 36.9 days + 28.7 days – 25.8 days
= 68.8 days

Task 8

(a)

Type of finance	Advantages
Bank loan	Relatively low cost
	Repayments can be negotiated
Overdraft	Security not normally required
	Useful to fund working capital
	Precise amount required does not need to be known
	Covenants not normally included

(b) The correct answer is

Freehold property	**Working capital**
Bank loan	Overdraft

(c)

	Increase overdraft ✓	Decrease overdraft ✓
Increase inventory levels	✓	
Improve credit control procedures		✓
Increase quantity of sales		✓
Drawings taken by the owner	✓	

Task 9

(i)   **Business risk**, the inherent risk of doing business for a company, refers to the risk of making only low profits, or even losses, due to the nature of the business that the company is involved in. A business which requires a high level of fixed costs and has a relatively low or volatile pattern of income or cash inflows may have trouble covering its payables including interest payments on debt, and so the level of business risk will be high. If fixed costs are low, and fairly easily covered, the business risk, in this aspect, will be low.

(ii)   A high level of debt creates **financial risk**. This is the risk of a company not being able to meet other obligations as a result of the need to make interest payments. The proportion of debt finance carried by a company is therefore as significant as the level of business risk. Financial risk can be seen from different points of view.

  (1)   **The company** as a whole. If a company's gearing ratio increases it may struggle to service the debt that it already has and will have difficulty raising new debt finance. If the company builds up debts that it cannot pay when they fall due, it will be forced into liquidation.

  (2)   **Lenders to the company**. From the lender's viewpoint, the interest rate charged on loan finance will normally reflect the risk associated with the loan and an assessment of a company's creditworthiness will be made. If a company cannot pay its debts, the company will go into liquidation owing its creditors money that they are unlikely to recover in full. This is particularly true in relation to unsecured loans and trade payables.

  (3)   **Ordinary shareholders**. A company will not make any dividend payments unless it is able to earn enough profit before interest and tax to pay all its interest charges, and then tax. The lower the profits or the higher the interest-bearing debts, the less there will be, if there is anything at all, for shareholders. This greater financial risk should be reflected in shareholders demanding a higher risk premium and therefore a higher cost of capital for the company.

Task 10

(a) Compliance with investment policy

	Risk high/med/low	Within company's maximum investment limit Yes/No	Annual Return %	Liquidity acceptable (1 month conversion) Yes/No?
Option 1	Medium	No	3.9%	Yes
Option 2	Low	Yes	3%	Yes
Option 3	Low	Yes	3.5%	Yes
Option 4	High	Yes	4.5%	Yes

Note. As Gilts are readily marketable securities they should be convertible into cash within 1 month.

All of the investment options have an acceptable level of liquidity, as they are all convertible to cash within 1 month. They also all satisfy the minimum return required of 3%.

Option 1 would be rejected for having too high a minimum investment value, and option 4 has a high level of risk.

Therefore the acceptable investments are options 2 and 3.

Investment strategy

Given the maximum investment requirement, the investment should be split between the options. The return from option 3 is higher than the return from option 2, therefore the recommended investment strategy is:

	Recommended Option (insert number)	Amount invested £	Total return £
Preferred Option	3	50,000	1,750
Next best Option	2	50,000	1,500
Total		100,000	3,250

Overall the company will earn a 3.25% return on its investment.

Working

3,250/100,000 = 3.25%

(b) **The main provisions of the UK Bribery Act 2010 include:**

- Giving a bribe ('active bribery') or receiving a bribe ('passive' bribery) are both offences.

- Bribing a public foreign official is an offence.

- What constitutes improper performance is judged by the 'reasonable person' in court.

- Companies have a duty to maintain adequate procedures so they can demonstrate they took reasonable efforts to prevent bribery.

- Reasonable hospitality is not an offence.

- Any officers of a business are also guilty of an offence if they consented or were involved with said offence.

BPP PRACTICE ASSESSMENT 3
CASH AND TREASURY MANAGEMENT

Time allowed: 2 hours and 30 minutes

Cash and Treasury Management (CTRM)
BPP practice assessment 3

Task 1

The cash budget for Jabes Ltd for the three months ended June has been partially completed. The following information is to be incorporated and the cash budget completed.

- Fixed production overheads are £25,000 per month. This includes depreciation of £5,000.

- Sales department costs are expected to be fixed at £12,000 per month including depreciation of £500 per month.

- The costs for the Speights Ltd's retail shop are fixed and are £7,000 per month including depreciation of £800.

- Administration overheads should be budgeted to be £25,000 each month.

- Overdraft interest is charged by the bank each month and should be budgeted at the rate of 1% per month on the overdrawn balance at the end of the previous month.

- All of the above costs are paid for in the month that they were incurred.

Using the additional information above, complete the cash budget for Jabes Ltd for the three months ending in June. Cash inflows should be entered as positive figures and cash outflows as negative figures. Zeroes must be entered where appropriate to achieve full marks.

	April £	May £	June £
Receipts:			
Total receipts – sales receipts	205,000	222,600	225,885
Payments:			
Payments to suppliers	–110,000	–66,000	–86,000
Payments for wages	–62,000	–57,500	–72,000
Fixed production overhead			
Sales department costs			
Shop costs			
Administration overheads			
Overdraft interest			
Total payments			
Net cash flow			
Bank balance b/f	–220,000		
Bank balance c/f			

Task 2

Lucent Ltd has been carrying out time series analysis on its sales volumes for the last three years. It wishes to use this time series analysis to forecast sales volumes for one of its shops which sells speciality products, for April, May and June 20X6.

The trend has been discovered to be a monthly increase of 20 units. In March 20X6 the trend figure for sales volume was 2,040 units. The time series analysis has also identified the following seasonal variations for months involved:

April	+43 units
May	+10 units
June	−25 units

The selling price of each unit is £12.

Monthly purchases are on average 60% of the value of sales.

(a) **Using the trend and monthly variations complete the table below to forecast the sales volume, sales value and purchases value for April, May and June 20X6.**

	Forecast trend	Variation	Forecast sales volume	Forecast sales £	Forecast purchases £
April					
May					
June					

Additional information

As well as time series analysis the business wants to forecast wages costs for the shop each period using an industry average wage rate index. The wages cost in March 20X6 was £10,200 when the wage rate index stood at 121. The forecast wage rate index for the next three months is as follows:

April	125
May	130
June	137

(b) **What will be the forecast wages cost for each of the months of April, May and June 20X6?**

Month	Wages cost £
April	
May	
June	

Task 3

A candle making company is preparing its cash budget for the three months ending June 20X6.

Production is expected to be 130,000 candles in April, 135,000 candles in May and 140,000 candles in June.

There is one unit of raw materials for each candle and there are currently 100,000 units of raw materials in the warehouse and it is intended to maintain inventory at this level.

The cost of raw materials for each candle is 60 pence. No price increase is expected in the budgetary period. All purchases are made in the month of production but not paid for until the following month. At 31 March 20X6 the payable for purchases made during March was £120,000.

(a) **Complete the table below to determine the raw materials purchases budget in both units and £ for each of the three months ending in June.**

	April Units	May Units	June Units
Production			
Opening inventory			
Closing inventory			
Purchases in units			
	£	£	£
Purchases in £			

(b) **Complete the table below to show the payments to suppliers for each of the three months ending in June.**

	April £	May £	June £
Opening payables			
April purchases			
May purchases			

Task 4

The cash budget for Magic Ltd for the three months ended December 20X1 has been partially completed. The following information is to be incorporated and the cash budget completed.

Additional information

- Capital expenditure of £24,000 should be budgeted for in October. This will give rise to additional depreciation of £200 per month which is to be included in production overheads.

- In addition to the depreciation mentioned above, production overheads are expected to be £14,000 per month.

- Repairs and maintenance costs should be budgeted at an average of £750 per month.

- The cash balance at 30 September 20X1 was £13,900.

- A dividend of £17,500 is due to be paid at the end of November.

- The Sales department is running a big advertising campaign in September. This is expected to cost £6,450 and will be paid for a month later.

Using the additional information above, complete the cash budget for Magic Ltd for the three months ending in December 20X1. Cash inflows should be entered as positive figures and cash outflows as negative figures. Zeroes must be entered where appropriate to achieve full marks.

Cash budget for three months ending 30 December 20X1

	October £	November £	December £
Receipts:			
Receipts from customers	**+89,400**	**+102,300**	**+93,600**
Payments:			
Payments to suppliers	–37,500	–45,600	–33,500
Wages	–22,000	–22,000	–22,000
Production overheads			
Advertising campaign			
Repairs and maintenance			
Capital expenditure			
Dividend			
Total payments			
Net cash flow			
Opening cash balance			
Closing cash balance			

Task 5

A business has prepared the following cash budget for three months ending 30 September 20X6.

	July £	August £	September £
Receipts:			
Receipts from customers	104,697	106,284	109,296
Payments:			
Payments to suppliers	−50,200	−52,600	−51,400
Wages	−21,300	−21,900	−23,700
Production overheads	−10,000	−10,500	−10,500
Selling overheads	−3,200	−3,200	−3,200
Repairs and maintenance	−2,500	−2,500	−2,500
Capital expenditure	0	−20,000	0
Total payments	−87,200	−110,700	−91,300
Net cash flow	17,497	−4,416	17,996
Opening cash balance	23,900	41,397	36,981
Closing cash balance	41,397	36,981	54,977

The following additional information has now come to light:

1   Suppliers are currently paid one month after the date of purchase (so the budgeted payment of £50,200 in July relates to June's purchases). To reduce material costs, from 1 July 20X6 the business intends to take advantage of a 5% discount by settling supplier invoices in the month of purchase. September purchases are expected to be £54,000.

2   Since preparing the budget the business has agreed to give the workers a 3% pay rise with effect from 1 August. Wages are paid in the month incurred.

3   A payment for advertising of £2,000 has been omitted from September's selling overheads.

4   Capital expenditure relates to a machine. The £500 increase in production overheads from August relates to depreciation on the new machine.

5   Interest is to be charged monthly, at a rate of 1%, on any overdraft at the start of the month.

Using the additional information above, complete the table below to show the revised cash budget for the three months ending September. Cash inflows should be entered as positive figures and cash outflows as negative figures. Zeroes must be entered where appropriate to achieve full marks.

	July £	August £	September £
Receipts:			
Receipts from customers	104,697	106,284	109,296
Payments:			
Payments to suppliers			
Wages			
Production overheads			
Selling overheads			
Repairs and maintenance	–2,500	–2,500	–2,500
Capital expenditure	0	–20,000	0
Interest on overdraft			
Total payments			
Net cash flow			
Opening cash balance	23,900		
Closing cash balance			

Task 6

The quarterly budget and actual figures for an organisation are provided below:

	Budgeted £	Actual £
Cash sales	22,500	28,600
Receipts from credit customers	104,000	98,760
Cash purchases	(10,800)	(7,400)
Payments to credit suppliers	(54,700)	(61,200)
Wages and salaries	(25,600)	(30,200)
General expenses	(24,600)	(20,300)
Capital expenditure	0	(20,000)
Net cash flows	**10,800**	**(11,740)**
Opening balance	2,500	2,500
Closing balance	**13,300**	**(9,240)**

(a) **Prepare a reconciliation of budgeted cash flow with actual cash flow for the quarter. Highlight the appropriate description for each entry. Use brackets to indicate figures which need to be subtracted in the reconciliation.**

	£
Budgeted closing cash balance	
Surplus/shortfall in cash sales	
Surplus/shortfall in receipts from credit customers	
Increase/decrease in cash payments	
Increase/decrease in payments to credit suppliers	
Increase/decrease in wages and salaries	
Increase/decrease in general expenses	
Increase/decrease in capital expenditure	
Actual cash balance	

(b) **Suggest a possible cause for the differences between budget and actual cash sales, receipts from credit customers, payments to credit suppliers, capital expenditure, and where appropriate suggest a possible course of action to control these variances.**

Task 7

The following financial information relates to PNP Co for the year just ended:

	£000
Turnover	5,242.0
Variable cost of sales	3,145.0
Inventory	603.0
Receivables	744.5
Payables	574.5

Segmental analysis of receivables

	Balance £	Average payment period	Discount	Bad debts £
Class 1	200,000	30 days	1.0%	none
Class 2	252,000	60 days	nil	12,600
Class 3	110,000	75 days	nil	11,000
Class 4	182,500	90 days	nil	21,900
	744,500			**45,500**

The receivable balances given are before taking account of irrecoverable debts. All sales are on credit. Production and sales take place evenly throughout the year. Current sales for each class of receivables are in proportion to their relative year-end balances before bad debts.

It has been proposed that the discount for early payment be increased from 1.0% to 1.5% for settlement within 30 days. It is expected that this will lead to 50% of existing Class 2 receivables becoming Class 1 receivables, as well as attracting new business worth £500,000 in turnover. The new business would be divided equally between Class 1 and Class 2 receivables. Fixed costs would not increase as a result of introducing the discount or by attracting new business. PNP finances receivables from an overdraft at an annual interest rate of 8%.

Calculate the current cash operating cycle

	days

and the revised cash operating cycle caused by increasing the discount for early payment.

	days

Task 8

A business is considering an expansion project and has been looking into financing options for this project. One option is a bank loan of £400,000 with an initial facility fee of 0.5% of the loan amount and annual interest fixed at 6.5% p.a. on the original loan principal. In order to fund the working capital required for the expansion the bank has also agreed an overdraft facility of £50,000 with an annual interest rate of 11%. The owners of the business believe that the average amount of the overdraft facility that will be used is £30,000 and this will only be for the last six months of the year.

(a) **Complete the table to show the total cost of this financing arrangement for the first year.**

	Workings	£
Facility fee		
Interest on loan		
Overdraft interest		
Total		

Assume the loan is to be taken out for a four year period and that the capital plus interest will be repaid in three equal annual instalments.

(b) **Complete the table to show the total interest cost over the life of the loan and the annual repayments split between interest and capital. Work to the nearest £.**

	Workings	£
Total loan interest		
Total repayment (capital plus interest)		
Annual repayment		
Of which: Capital element		
Interest element		

(c) **Select from the picklists to complete the sentences below:**

The longer the period you wish to invest surplus cash for, the (1) [▼] the available interest rate is likely to be. Gilts are more suitable for (2) [▼] investments and the interest rate on them is usually (3) [▼] . Treasury Bills, issued by the (4) [▼] are (5) [▼] investments which (6) [▼] be traded. Gilts and Treasury stock are considered to be (7) [▼] investments and as a result will offer a (8) [▼] rate of return than an investment in equity shares.

Picklist:

(1) higher/lower
(2) short term/long term
(3) fixed/variable
(4) stock exchange/government/local authority
(5) short term/long term
(6) can/cannot
(7) high risk/low risk
(8) higher/lower

(d) An investment of £500,000 is made in a money market account which pays interest of 2.8% per annum.

How much interest will be received if the investment is held for 3 months?

£ [   ]

(e) A company purchases gilts with a nominal value of £100,000 for a price of £94,000.

On maturity the company will receive £94,000.

Is this statement true or false?

	✓
True	
False	

Task 9

(a) **Explain the difference between an overdraft and a loan and the circumstances when each might be used.**

(b) A company has an aggressive approach to working capital management, whereby all fluctuating assets (assets held over and above the minimum amounts) plus a certain proportion of permanent current assets are financed by short-term capital such as bank overdrafts and trade payables.

What could be the problems of this approach and what alternative financing sources could the company consider?

Task 10

A company has forecast that it has £50,000 available to invest for six months before the capital will be required to construct a new factory.

It is considering the following three options:

Option 1:

Invest in a mixed portfolio of shares and treasury stock. The minimum period of investment is 6 months; interest rate is 6% p.a.

Option 2:

Invest in a certificate of deposit with a six month term; interest rate is 4.5% p.a.

Option 3:

Investment in a deposit account; interest rate is 5% p.a. There is a penalty of 0.5% of capital invested for withdrawal before 12 months.

(a) **Draft an email to the financial director of the company assessing the investment options and recommending a course of action.**

The company investment policy includes full compliance with Money Laundering regulations.

(b) **Outline in an email to the finance director what they basic provisions of money laundering legislation are, and how they might apply to choosing where to invest surplus funds.**

BPP PRACTICE ASSESSMENT 3
CASH AND TREASURY MANAGEMENT

ANSWERS

Cash and Treasury Management (CTRM)
BPP practice assessment 3

Task 1

Cash budget for the three months ended 30 June 20X6

	April £	May £	June £
Receipts:			
Total receipts – sales receipts	205,000	222,600	225,885
Payments:			
Payments to suppliers	–110,000	–66,000	–86,000
Payments for wages	–62,000	–57,500	–72,000
Fixed production overhead	–20,000	–20,000	–20,000
Sales department costs	–11,500	–11,500	–11,500
Shop costs	–6,200	–6,200	–6,200
Administration overheads	–25,000	–25,000	–25,000
Overdraft interest	–2,200	–2,519	–2,180
Total payments	**–236,900**	**–188,719**	**–222,880**
Net cash flow	**–31,900**	**33,881**	**3,005**
Bank balance b/f	**–220,000**	**–251,900**	**–218,019**
Bank balance c/f	**–251,900**	**–218,019**	**–215,014**

Task 2

(a)

	Forecast trend	Variation	Forecast sales volume	Forecast sales £	Forecast purchases £
April	2,060	+43	2,103	25,236	15,142
May	2,080	+10	2,090	25,080	15,048
June	2,100	−25	2,075	24,900	14,940

(b)

Month	Wages cost £
April 10,200 × 125/121	10,537
May 10,200 × 130/121	10,959
June 10,200 × 137/121	11,549

Task 3

(a) Purchases budget

	April Units	May Units	June Units
Production	130,000	135,000	140,000
Opening inventory	−100,000	−100,000	−100,000
Closing inventory	100,000	100,000	100,000
Purchases in units	**130,000**	**135,000**	**140,000**
	£	£	£
Purchases in £ (units × £0.60)	**78,000**	**81,000**	**84,000**

(b) Payments to suppliers

	April £	May £	June £
Opening payables	120,000		
April purchases		78,000	
May purchases			81,000

Task 4

Cash budget for three months ending 30 December 20X1

	October £	November £	December £
Receipts:			
Receipts from customers	**+89,400**	**+102,300**	**+93,600**
Payments:			
Payments to suppliers	–37,500	–45,600	–33,500
Wages	–22,000	–22,000	–22,000
Production overheads	–14,000	–14,000	–14,000
Advertising campaign	–6,450		
Repairs and maintenance	–750	–750	–750
Capital expenditure	–24,000		
Dividend		–17,500	
Total payments	**–104,700**	**–99,850**	**70,250**
Net cash flow	–15,300	+2,450	+23,350
Opening cash balance	+13,900	–1,400	+1,050
Closing cash balance	–1,400	+1,050	+24,400

Task 5

	July £	August £	September £
Receipts:			
Receipts from customers	104,697	106,284	109,296
Payments:			
Payments to suppliers June purchases (1 month credit) July purchases (52,600 × 0.95) August purchases (51,400 × 0.95) September purchases (54,000 × 0.95)	−50,200 −49,970	−48,830	−51,300
Wages 21,300 21,900 × 1.03 23,700 × 1.03	−21,300	−22,557	−24,411
Production overheads	−10,000	−10,000	−10,000
Selling overheads	−3,200	−3,200	−5,200
Repairs and maintenance	−2,500	−2,500	−2,500
Capital expenditure	0	−20,000	0
Interest on overdraft	0	−86	−95
Total payments	−137,170	−107,173	−93,506
Net cash flow	−32,473	−889	15,790
Opening cash balance	23,900	−8,573	−9,462
Closing cash balance	**−8,573**	**−9,462**	**6,328**

Task 6

(a)

	£
Budgeted closing cash balance	13,300
Surplus in cash sales	6,100
Shortfall in receipts from credit customers	−5,240
Decrease in cash payments	3,400
Increase in payments to credit suppliers	−6,500
Increase in wages and salaries	−4,600
Decrease in general expenses	4,300
Increase in capital expenditure	−20,000
Actual cash balance	**−9,240**

(b)

Surplus of cash sales	Higher overall sales, or a lower price (settlement discount) offered for immediate receipt of cash.
	This is a beneficial variance, so the company may seek to enhance these rather than control them, however, if a discount is being offered for cash payment, care should be taken to ensure that the values of the discount compared to the cost of financing the credit term is financially worthwhile.
Shortfall in receipts from credit customers	This could be caused by sales being made for cash rather than on credit, customers taking longer to pay, or a key customer goes into liquidation.
	Longer payment periods can be managed by improving credit control, and while customer liquidations are outside the control of the company to a certain extent, the continued monitoring of customers creditworthiness can indicate problems in advance and steps could be taken to limit or stop the credit offered.

Increase in payments to credit suppliers	Payments to suppliers being made earlier, bulk buying arrangements or unexpected increase in production requirements.
	Whether or not this is a problem depends on the reasons for this taking place – if payments are being made early to take advantage of beneficial early payment or bulk discounts, then these are worthwhile. If however the payments are simply taking place earlier than required, this could be damaging to the liquidity needs of the company and should be curtailed.
Increase in capital expenditure	Unexpected breakdown of necessary machinery which cannot be repaired or capital expenditure which has not been budgeted for is being incurred.
	Improve budgeting procedures would control the unbudgeted expenditure issue.

Task 7

Current cash operating cycle: 55 days

Inventory days = 603/3,145 × 365 = 70 days
Payables days = 574.5/3,145 × 365 = 67 days
Receivables days = 744.5/5,242 × 365 = 52 days
Cash operating cycle = 70 + 52 − 67 = 55 days

Revised cash operating cycle: 54 days

Following the implementation of the increased discount for early payment, total receivables will increase by £61,644 to £806,144 and turnover will have increased to £5,742,000. This results in a slight fall in receivable days to 51 days (806,144/5,742,000 × 365) and therefore a slight fall of one day in the cash operating cycle to 54 days.

Workings

Total receivables increase
£250,000/(365/30) = £20,548
£250,000/(365/60) = £41,096
Turnover
£5,242,000 + £500,000 = £5,742,000

Task 8

(a)

	Workings	£
Facility fee	0.5% × £400,000	2,000
Interest on loan	6.5% × £400,000	26,000
Overdraft interest	11% × 30,000 × 6/12	1,650
Total		29,650

(b)

	Workings	£
Total loan interest	6.5% × 400,000 × 4	104,000
Total repayment (capital plus interest)	400,000 + 104,000	504,000
Annual repayment	504,000/3	168,000
Of which: Capital element	400,000/3	133,333
Interest element	104,000/3	34,667

(c) The longer the period you wish to invest surplus cash for, the
(1) [higher] the available interest rate is likely to be. Gilts are more
suitable for (2) [long term] investments and the interest rate on them
is usually (3) [fixed]. Treasury Bills, issued by the
(4) [government] are (5) [short term] investments which
(6) [can] be traded. Gilts and Treasury stock are considered to
be (7) [low risk] investments and as a result will offer a
(8) [lower] rate of return than an investment in equity shares.

(d) £500,000 × 2.8% × 3/12 = £3,500

(e) False. The company will receive the nominal value of £100,000.

Task 9

(a) An overdraft will tend to have a higher rate of interest than a bank loan. The interest will be charged on the amount of the facility used. An overdraft is repayable on demand and is particularly useful for funding working capital or for short-term finance requirements eg due to seasonality.

A bank loan will be for a fixed term and interest will be charged on the whole amount, regardless of how much of the funds are used. A loan may have covenants attached to it by the lender. In addition the lender may require security in the form of a charge on the assets of the business. There are two types of charge which could be required, a floating charge is a charge on the current assets of the company – the company can buy and sell the assets on which the floating charge is secured. A fixed charge is a charge on a specific asset and the company is not permitted to sell the asset without discharging the debt beforehand.

A loan would normally be used for the purchase of non-current assets. The term of the bank loan should be matched with the life of the assets that it finances, so that the income generated can be used for debt servicing.

(b) Aggressive management

Current assets can be broken down into two portions, **permanent** current assets and **fluctuating** current assets. The permanent current assets represent base levels of inventories, receivables, etc., that will always be on hand. Fluctuating current assets represent the seasonal build-ups that occur, such as inventories before Christmas and receivables after Christmas.

There is no problem financing fluctuating current assets with short-term finance as a business does not want to pay financing charges all year if it only needs the money for a short period.

The permanent current assets are, individually, short life assets, but they represent minimum balances that will always need to be financed. While it is possible to finance permanent working capital needs with short-term debt, it is risky to do so:

Short-term interest rates fluctuate much more than long-term interest rates. Also if the company has a bad year it may find that lenders are unwilling to continue to extend the overdraft.

Thus aggressive management will mean that there is an increased risk of cash flow and liquidity problems.

Businesses may also suffer higher interest costs on short-term sources of finance.

Alternative financing

It is less risky if permanent current assets are financed long-term, like non-current assets.

If short-term methods cannot be used, long-term funding such as long-term loans or share capital not tied up in funding non-current assets will be used to support working capital. This will mean that working capital is managed conservatively, with all non-current assets and permanent current assets, as well as part of fluctuating current assets, being financed by long-term capital. When fluctuating current assets are low, there will be surplus cash which the company will be able to invest in marketable securities.

Task 10

(a)

> Email
>
> **To**: fd@company.co.uk   **Date**:   Today
>
> **From**: aatstudent@company.co.uk   **Subject**:   Investment options
>
> The company has £50,000 to invest for a period of six months. As the investment is required for the construction of the factory, it is important that we do not expose the company to capital risk.
>
> If the company selects Option 1, the total return on the investment will be £1,500.
>
> If the company selects Option 2, the total return on the investment will be £1,125.
>
> If the company selects Option 3, the total return on the investment will be £1,000.
>
> I recommend that Option 2 be selected as this will have the lowest risk for the company. The investment will earn a return, after six months, of 2.25 %.

Workings

Option 1: £50,000 × 6% × 6/12 = £1,500

Option 2: £50,000 × 4.5% × 6/12 = £1,125

Option 3: £50,000 × 5% × 6/12 = £1,250 less penalty for early withdrawal £250 (0.5% × £50,000) = £1,000

(b)

Email

To: fd@company.co.uk   **Date**:   Today

From: aatstudent@company.co.uk   **Subject**:   Investment options

The main provisions of money laundering regulations are:

It is illegal to hide the proceeds of crime or move it offshore. We should be sure the funds we are looking to invest are from an identified and legitimate source – I am sure they are but we would do well to check and evidence this.

It is also an offence to be part of any offence that allows others access to criminal property.

Finally, it is an offence to acquire property which is known or suspected to be the proceeds of a crime.

In relation to the last two points we should ensure the securities we purchase are from a legitimate source and we should satisfy ourselves they are not instrumental in helping criminals to legitimise the proceeds of crime.

BPP PRACTICE ASSESSMENT 4
CASH AND TREASURY MANAGEMENT

Time allowed: 2 hours and 30 minutes

Cash and Treasury Management (CTRM)
BPP practice assessment 4

Task 1

(a) Complete the table from the lists below by filling in a description of the type of payment and suggesting three transactions for each type of payment.

Type of payment	Description	Example transactions
Discretionary		
Non-discretionary		

(b) The statement of profit or loss of a business for the three months ended 31 December shows that there is sales revenue of £175,000.

Extracts from the sales ledger control account at 1 October and 31 December show the following balances:

	31 December	1 October
Trade receivables	£60,500	£64,000

Drag and drop the entries to the correct position to complete the sales ledger control account then enter the correct figure for the cash received from customers in the period:

Balance b/d
Balance c/d
Sales
60,500
64,000
175,000

Sales ledger control account

	Dr £		Cr £
		Cash received (balancing figure)	

Task 2

(a) You are given an extract from a company's records about the average hourly wage rate.

Complete the table to show the wage rate index for each month.

	Actual hourly wage rate	Wage rate Index
January	£6.00	100
February	£6.36	
March	£6.48	
April	£6.72	
May	£6.72	
June	£6.84	

(b) Each unit of product requires 3 hours of labour and the production budget for July is to manufacture 12,500 units.

If the index for July is 115 what is the budgeted payment for labour hours?

Payment for July labour hours

£ [   ]

The trend figures for sales in £ for a business for the four quarters of last year and the seasonal variations are estimated as:

	Trend sales £	Seasonal variations
Quarter 1	160,000	+12,820
Quarter 2	164,500	+14,805
Quarter 3	169,000	–5,070
Quarter 4	173,500	–22,555

(c) **Assuming the trend continues, complete the table to show the forecast sales for each of the four quarters of next year.**

	This year's trend sales £	Additive adjustment for seasonal variation	Sales budget
Quarter 1			
Quarter 2			
Quarter 3			
Quarter 4			

(d) The overhead costs of a company have been found to be accurately represented by the formula:

$y = £10,000 + £0.25x$

where y is the monthly cost and x represents the activity level measured as the number of orders.

Monthly activity levels of orders may be estimated using a combined regression analysis and time series model:

$a = 100,000 + 30b$

where a represents the de-seasonalised monthly activity level and b represents the month number.

In month 240, the seasonal index value is 108.

Calculate the overhead cost for month 240 to the nearest £1,000.

Task 3

A business buys handbags from a wholesaler and then sells them to customers, in the same month, at a mark-up of 60% on cost.

30% of the sales are cash and 70% are on credit. 80% of credit customers pay one month later and the remaining 20% pay 2 months after the date of sale.

Complete the tables below to show the total sales for the three months from October to December, the split between cash and credit sales, the timing of cash receipts and the trade receivables at the end of December. Round to whole £'s throughout and enter zeroes where appropriate.

	October £	November £	December £
Purchases of handbags	120,000	130,000	140,000
Total sales			
Split:			
Cash sales			
Credit sales			

294

	Workings	Oct cash received £	Nov cash received £	Dec cash received £	y/e trade receivables £
Cash sales					
Cash from credit sales:					
October					
October					
November					
November					
December					
Total					

Task 4

Property Co has been in business for only a short time and is preparing a cash budget for the first four months of 20X6. Expected sales are as follows.

	20X5	20X6	20X6	20X6	20X6
Month	December	January	February	March	April
Units sold	10	10	15	25	30

The average price of each unit is £5,400 and Property Co receives 1/3 of its income in the month of sale and the remaining 2/3 in the month after sale. The company has nine employees who are paid on a monthly basis. The average salary per employee is £35,000 per year. If more than 20 units are sold in a given month, each employee is paid in that month a bonus of £140 for each additional unit sold.

Variable expenses are incurred at the rate of 16.67% of the value of each unit sold and these expenses are paid in the month of sale. Fixed overheads of £4,300 per month are paid in the month in which they arise. The company pays interest every three months on a loan of £200,000 at a simple interest rate of 6% per year. The last interest payment in each year is paid in December.

An outstanding tax liability of £95,800 is due to be paid in April. In the same month the company intends to dispose of surplus vehicles, with a carrying value of £15,000, for £20,000. The cash balance at the start of January 20X6 is expected to be a deficit of £40,000.

Prepare a monthly cash budget for the period from January to April 20X6. Your budget must clearly indicate each item of income and expenditure, and the opening and closing monthly cash balances.

	Jan £000	Feb £000	March £000	April £000
Receipts:				
Fee on sale				
Receipt on sale of vehicles				
Total receipts				
Payments:				
Salaries				
Bonus				
Variable expenses				
Fixed overheads				
Interest on loan				
Tax liability				
Total payments				
Net cash flow				
Balance b/fwd				
Balance c/fwd				

Task 5

A business needs help deciding whether or not to introduce a prompt payment discount in order to collect cash from its credit customers in sooner.

The sales budget is as follows:

	£
Period 1 sales	144,000
Period 2 sales	151,500
Period 3 sales	145,450
Period 4 sales	139,000
Period 5 sales	162,300

The original cash receipts budget was prepared assuming that 60% of sales were paid for by customers in the month following the sale and the remaining 37% of customers paid two months after the sale, with 3% of all debts remaining uncollected.

	Period 3 £	Period 4 £	Period 5 £
Period 1 sales £144,000 × 37%	53,280		
Period 2 sales £151,500 × 60%	90,900		
Period 2 sales £151,500 × 37%		56,055	
Period 3 sales £145,450 × 60%		87,270	
Period 3 sales £145,450 × 37%			53,817
Period 4 sales £139,000 × 60%			83,400
Total receipts from customers	**144,180**	**143,325**	**137,217**

The company is considering introducing a settlement discount at the start of period 3. The discount will be 2% for payments made in the month of the sale. This policy is expected to result in 40% of customers paying in the month of the sale, 30% paying in the month following the sale and the remaining 30% paying two months following the sale. As cash is being collected faster, the company is expecting to eliminate irrecoverable debts. It also expects sales to increase by 5% from period 3 because more customers will be attracted by the change in credit policy.

(a) Complete the table below to calculate the forecast receipts from customers for each of periods 3, 4 and 5 if the system of settlement discounts is introduced.

	Workings	Period 3 £	Period 4 £	Period 5 £
Period 1 sales				
Period 2 sales				
Period 2 sales				
Period 3 sales				
Period 3 sales				
Period 3 sales				
Period 4 sales				
Period 4 sales				
Period 5 sales				
Total receipts from customers				

(b) Complete the tables below to show the effects of introducing the discount system.

	Period 3 £	Period 4 £	Period 5 £
Original receipts from customers			
Revised receipts from customers			
Overall increase/(decrease) in sales receipts			

Cost of prompt payment discount	Workings	Period 3 £	Period 4 £	Period 5 £
Period 3 sales				
Period 4 sales				
Period 5 sales				

Task 6

The quarterly budget and actual figures for an organisation are provided below.

(a) **Complete the table to show the variance arising and use a + or – to indicate whether it is favourable or adverse.**

	Budgeted cash flows £	Actual cash flows £	Variance £
Cash sales	32,500	28,600	
Receipts from credit customers	234,000	198,760	
Sale of machinery	0	7,500	
Payments to credit suppliers	(124,700)	(91,200)	
Wages and salaries	(35,600)	(30,200)	
General expenses	(14,600)	(10,300)	
Capital expenditure	0	(20,000)	
Drawings	(30,000)	(35,000)	
Net cash flows	**61,600**	**48,160**	
Opening balance	32,500	32,500	
Closing balance	**94,100**	**80,660**	

(b) **Explain what impact the following situations might have on the cash budget.**

Some customers, who previously bought goods on credit, are taking advantage of lower prices offered on cash sales	
A machine needed to be replaced unexpectedly when it broke down	
Material costs have decreased	
Large orders necessitated additional overtime working	

Task 7

(a) **Which one of the following equations best describes the cash operating cycle?**

average inventory holding period + average trade payables' payment period – average trade receivables' collection period ☐

average inventory holding period + average trade receivables' collection period – average trade payables' payment period ☐

average cash balance + average trade receivables' collection period – average trade payables' payment period ☐

average cash balance – average trade receivables' collection period + average trade payables' payment period ☐

(b) **Which of the following should a business do in order to improve its cash operating cycle?**

Increase inventories of raw material ☐

Decrease the credit period taken from trade suppliers ☐

Extend the credit period for customers ☐

Reduce the time taken to produce its product ☐

(c) A company's current cash operating cycle is 34 days.

Which of the following will have the effect of reducing the cash operating cycle?

Increasing the inventory holding period by 3 days ☐

Decreasing the trade payables' payment period by 5 days ☐

Decreasing the trade receivables' collection period by 2 days ☐

Increasing the average cash balance by 10% ☐

(d) A company wishes to minimise its inventory costs. Annual demand for a raw material costing £12 per unit is 60,000 units per year. Inventory management costs for this raw material are as follows:

Ordering cost: £6 per order

The supplier of this raw material has offered a bulk purchase discount of 1% for order quantities of 10,000 units or more.

Calculate the cost of inventory if the discount is taken up.

£ _____

Task 8

A company has forecast the balance on the business bank account at the end of each of the next 6 months. Brackets indicate overdrawn balances. The company's business is seasonal and, after June, the bank account is expected to remain in credit for the remainder of the year.

Month	£
January	3,950
February	(6,700)
March	(11,200)
April	(2,400)
May	(10,800)
June	1,250

The company has contacted the bank and has been offered the following options:

Option 1

Arrange a bank overdraft. There Is an arrangement fee of £500 to be paid in January, and interest will be charged at 12% per annum. Interest is to be calculated and charged monthly.

Option 2

Arrange a short term bank loan for the year of £12,000, with an interest rate of 8%, to be repaid in equal monthly instalments.

(a) **Complete the tables below to ascertain the cost of the two options:**

Option 1:

For the purposes of the calculation assume interest is to be charged on the forecast bank balance at the end of each month in which the overdraft is used.

Option 1:

	Month-end balance £	Overdraft cost £
January	3,950	
February	(6,700)	
March	(11,200)	
April	(2,400)	
May	(10,800)	
June	1,250	
Total cost		

Option 2:

	£
Total annual interest	
Monthly interest payment (Jan–Dec)	

(b) **Complete the gap fills and select from the picklists to complete the draft email to the finance director of the company:**

Email

To: [▼]   **Date**:   Today

From: [▼]   **Subject**: Raising finance

The information supplied indicates that the company will have a maximum

overdrawn balance of £ [_____] during the year.

If the company selects the overdraft option, the cost for the year will be

£ [_____] ,whereas the annual cost of the short term bank loan is

£ [_____] .

I recommend that the [▼] option be selected as this will have the

[▼] cost for the company. As the business is seasonal, the

[▼] provides the [▼] . Although the interest rate on the

loan is [▼] , interest has to be paid for [_____] months,

despite the business bank account being [▼] for more than six

months of the year.

Picklist:

fd@company.co.uk   aatstudent@company.co.uk
bank overdraft   short term bank loan
highest   lowest
bank overdraft   short term bank loan
most flexibility   least flexibility
lower   higher
in credit   overdrawn

Task 9

In looking to reduce the working capital funding requirement, the financial controller of your company is considering factoring credit sales. The company's annual turnover is £2.5m of which 90% are credit sales. On average customers take 2.5 months to pay. Irrecoverable debts are typically 3% of credit sales.

The salary of the Receivables Ledger Administrator is £12,500 and this would be saved under the proposals. The company's cost of overdraft finance is 12% per annum.

Write a report to the financial controller that outlines the benefits of factoring. Include in your report a calculation of the existing receivable collection costs.

Task 10

Discuss the factors to be considered by the company when planning ways to invest any cash surplus forecast by its cash budgets.

BPP PRACTICE ASSESSMENT 4
CASH AND TREASURY MANAGEMENT

ANSWERS

Cash and Treasury Management (CTRM)
BPP practice assessment 4

Task 1

(a)

Type of payment	Description	Example transactions
Discretionary	Payments which can validly be cancelled or delayed	Drawings Training costs Capital expenditure
Non-discretionary	Payments which must be made on time for the business to continue	PAYE and NI due to HM Revenue and Customs Payment to credit suppliers Annual loan interest

(b) Sales ledger control account

	Dr £		Cr £
Balance b/d	64,000		
Sales	175,000	Cash received (239,000 – 60,500)	178,500
		Balance c/d	60,500
	£239,000		£239,000

Task 2

(a)

	Actual hourly wage rate	Wage rate Index
January	£6.00	100
February	£6.36	106
March	£6.48	108
April	£6.72	112
May	£6.72	112
June	£6.84	114

(b)

Payment for July labour hours	£258,750 (12500 × 3 × £6.00 × 1.15)

(c)

	This year's trend sales £	Additive adjustment for seasonal variation	Sales budget
Quarter 1	178,000	+ 12,820	190,820
Quarter 2	182,500	+ 14,805	197,305
Quarter 3	187,000	−5,070	181,930
Quarter 4	191,500	−22,555	168,945

(d) £39,000

The overhead cost is represented by

$y = £10,000 + £0.25x$ where x = number of orders

Orders are estimated as follows, using the given formula which combines regression analysis and a time series model.

Number of orders = (100,000 + (240 × 30)) × Index value
= (100,000 + 7,200) × 1.08
= 115,776

Using $y = £10,000 + £0.25x$ where x = number of orders = 115,776

The overhead cost is therefore = £10,000 + (£0.25 × 115,776) = £38,944

= £39,000 to the nearest £1,000.

Task 3

	October £	November £	December £
Purchases	120,000	130,000	140,000
Total sales	**192,000**	**208,000**	**224,000**
Split:			
Cash sales (30%)	57,600	62,400	67,200
Credit sales (70%)	134,400	145,600	156,800

	Workings	Oct cash received £	Nov cash received £	Dec cash received £	y/e trade receivables £
Cash sales		57,600	62,400	67,200	
Cash from Credit sales:					
October	134,400 × 80%	0	107,520	0	0
October	134,400 × 20%	0	0	26,880	0
November	145,600 × 80%		0	116,480	0
November	145,600 × 20%		0	0	29,120
December	156,800 × 100%	0	0	0	156,800
Total		**57,600**	**169,920**	**210,560**	**185,920**

Task 4

Cash budget

	Jan £000	Feb £000	March £000	April £000
Receipts:				
Fee on sale (W1)	54	63	99	144
Receipt on sale of vehicles				20
Total receipts	**54**	**63**	**99**	**164**
Payments:				
Salaries (9 × £35,000/12)	26.25	26.25	26.25	26.25
Bonus (W2)			6.3	12.6
Variable expenses (W3)	9	13.5	22.5	27
Fixed overheads	4.3	4.3	4.3	4.3
Interest on loan			3.0	
Tax liability				95.80
Total payments	**39.55**	**44.05**	**62.35**	**165.95**
Net cash flow	**14.45**	**18.95**	**36.65**	**(1.95)**
Balance b/fwd	(40.00)	(25.55)	(6.6)	30.05
Balance c/fwd	**(25.55)**	**(6.6)**	**30.05**	**28.10**

Workings

1

	Jan	Feb	March	April
Receipts				
Unit sales	10	15	25	30
	£000	£000	£000	£000
Income (£5,400 × numbers sold)	54	81	135	162
Received				
– 1/3 in month of sale	18	27	45	54
– 2/3 in following month				
(January receipt relates to December sale)	36	36	54	90
Total income in the month	**54**	**63**	**99**	**144**

2

	Jan	Feb	March	April
Unit sales	10	15	25	30
	£000	£000	£000	£000
Bonus based on numbers sold over 20	0	0	5	10
– £140 × 9 × numbers sold over 20	0	0	6.3	12.6

3

	Jan	Feb	March	April
Income	54	81	135	162
	£000	£000	£000	£000
Variable overheads at 16.67%	9	13.5	22.5	27

Task 5

(a)

	Workings	Period 3 £	Period 4 £	Period 5 £
Period 1 sales	£144,000 × 37%	53,280		
Period 2 sales	£151,500 × 60%	90,900		
Period 2 sales	£151,500 × 37%		56,055	
Period 3 sales	£145,450 × 1.05 × 40% × 98%	59,867		
Period 3 sales	£145,450 × 1.05 × 30%		45,817	
Period 3 sales	£145,450 × 1.05 × 30%			45,817
Period 4 sales	£139,000 × 1.05 × 40% × 98%		57,212	
Period 4 sales	£139,000 × 1.05 × 30%			43,785
Period 5 sales	£162,300 × 1.05 × 40% × 98%			66,803
Total receipts from customers		**204,047**	**159,084**	**156,405**

(b)

	Period 3 £	Period 4 £	Period 5 £
Original receipts from customers	144,180	143,325	137,217
Revised receipts from customers	204,047	159,084	156,405
Overall increase/(decrease) in sales receipts	**+59,867**	**+15,759**	**+19,188**

Cost of prompt payment discount	Workings	Period 3 £	Period 4 £	Period 5 £
Period 3 sales	£145,450 × 1.05 × 40% × 2%	−1,222		
Period 4 sales	£139,000 × 1.05 × 40% × 2%		−1,168	
Period 5 sales	£162,300 × 1.05 × 40% × 2%			−1,363

Task 6

(a)

	Budgeted cash flows £	Actual cash flows £	Variance £
Cash sales	32,500	28,600	−3,900
Receipts from credit customers	234,000	198,760	−35,240
Sale of machinery	0	7,500	+7,500
Payments to credit suppliers	(124,700)	(91,200)	+33,500
Wages and salaries	(35,600)	(30,200)	+5,400
General expenses	(14,600)	(10,300)	+4,300
Capital expenditure	0	(20,000)	−20,000
Drawings	(30,000)	(35,000)	−5,000
Net cash flows	**61,600**	**48,160**	**−13,440**
Opening balance	32,500	32,500	0
Closing balance	**94,100**	**80,660**	**−13,440**

(b)

Some customers, who previously bought goods on credit, are taking advantage of lower prices offered on cash sales	Reduction in receipts from credit sales
A machine needed to be replaced unexpectedly when it broke down	Increased capital expenditure
Material costs have decreased	Reduction in payments to suppliers
Large orders necessitated additional overtime working	Increased payments for wages

Task 7

(a) average inventory holding period + average trade receivables' collection period – average trade payables' payment period

(b) Reduce the time taken to produce its product as this will reduce the inventory holding period

(c) Decreasing the trade receivables' collection period by 2 days

(d) Order size for bulk discounts is 10,000

Number of orders per year	= 60,000/10,000 = 6
Annual ordering cost	= 6 × £6 = £36
Inventory cost	= 60,000 × £12 × 99% = £712,800
Total cost of inventory with discount	= 712,800 + 36 = £712,836

Task 8

(a) **Option 1:**

	Month-end balance £	Overdraft cost £
January	3,950	500
February	(6,700)	67
March	(11,200)	112
April	(2,400)	24
May	(10,800)	108
June	1,250	0
Total cost		**811**

Option 2:

	£
Total interest	960
Monthly interest payment (Jan–Dec)	80

(b)

Email

To: [fd@company.co.uk]   **Date**:   Today

From: [aatstudent@company.co.uk]   **Subject**:   Raising finance

The information supplied indicates that the company will have a maximum overdrawn balance of £ [11,300] during the year.

If the company selects the overdraft option the cost for the year will be £ [811], whereas the annual cost of the short term bank loan is £ [960].

I recommend that the [bank overdraft] option be selected as this will have the [lowest] cost for the company. As the business is seasonal the [bank overdraft] provides the [most flexibility]. Although the interest rate on the loan is [lower], interest has to be paid for [12] months, despite the business bank account being [in credit] for more than six months of the year.

Task 9

To: Financial Controller
From: Adviser
Subject: Working capital
Date: 27 September 20X2

This report covers the benefits of factoring

Benefits of factoring

(1)   The business can pay its suppliers promptly, and so be able to take advantage of any early payment discounts that are available.

(2)   Optimum inventory levels can be maintained, because the business will have enough cash to pay for the inventories it needs.

(3)   Growth can be financed through sales rather than by injecting fresh external capital.

(4)   The business gets finance linked to its volume of sales. In contrast, overdraft limits tend to be determined by historical balance sheets.

(5) The managers of the business do not have to spend their time on the problems of slow paying receivables and with non-recourse factoring the risk of irrecoverable debts lies with the factor.

(6) The business does not incur the costs of running its own sales ledger department, and can use the expertise of receivable management that the factor has.

(7) Because they are managing a number of sales ledgers, factors can manage receivables more efficiently than individual businesses through economies of scale.

Existing receivables collection costs

	£
Irrecoverable debts (3% × 90% × £2.5m)	67,500
Salary of sales ledger administrator	12,500
Cost of financing debts (90% × (2.5/12) × 12% × £2.5m)	56,250
Total cost	136,250

Task 10

Factors to consider when investing any cash surplus

The cash budget for Property Co shows an increase in sales over the period, which suggests higher sales as the spring approaches. However, the payment of tax in April means that a trend of increasing net cash flows is temporarily reversed.

The company needs to consider the following when investing any surpluses:

(i) Short-term investments with no capital risk would be suitable as these may be called upon at any time. Short-term investments include bank deposit accounts, certificates of deposit, term bills and gilts, which are short-dated. In choosing between these, the company will need to consider the size of the surplus, the length of time it is available, the yield offered and the risk associated with each instrument.

(ii) On an annual basis, look at any surpluses and invest these in longer-term higher yield assets. The company will most probably call on these at some stage to fund expansion but needs to pick the investments carefully.

The investment of cash balances is part of the treasury function of a company. It is unlikely that Property Co is of a size to sustain a full time treasury activity but nonetheless there is a definite benefit in closely managing any surpluses.

In addition, ethics and sustainability should be considered. If the funds are placed in an ethically questionable or unsustainable investment, this could affect Property Co in several ways:

- Lose customers if they find out and are concerned with the issue

- Demotivate employees

- Lose suppliers and providers of finance if they wish to disassociate themselves from us to protect their reputation